D0977088

Little Bites of Big Data
for Public Policy

Sara Miller McCune founded SAGE Publishing in 1965 to support the dissemination of usable knowledge and educate a global community. SAGE publishes more than 1000 journals and over 800 new books each year, spanning a wide range of subject areas. Our growing selection of library products includes archives, data, case studies and video. SAGE remains majority owned by our founder and after her lifetime will become owned by a charitable trust that secures the company's continued independence.

Los Angeles | London | New Delhi | Singapore | Washington DC | Melbourne

Little Bites of Big Data for Public Policy

Donald F. Kettl

University of Maryland

FOR INFORMATION:

CQ Press

An imprint of SAGE Publications, Inc.

2455 Teller Road

Thousand Oaks, California 91320

E-mail: order@sagepub.com

SAGE Publications Ltd.

1 Oliver's Yard

55 City Road

London EC1Y 1SP

United Kingdom

SAGE Publications India Pvt. Ltd.

B 1/I 1 Mohan Cooperative Industrial Area

Mathura Road, New Delhi 110 044

India

SAGE Publications Asia-Pacific Pte. Ltd.

3 Church Street

#10-04 Samsung Hub

Singapore 049483

Copyright © 2018 by CQ Press, an imprint of SAGE. CQ Press is a registered trademark of Congressional Quarterly Inc.

All rights reserved. No part of this publication may be reproduced or transmitted in any form or by any means, electronic or mechanical, including photocopy, recording, or any information storage and retrieval system, without permission in writing from the publisher.

Printed in the United States of America.

ISBN: 978-1-5063-8352-1

This book is printed on acid-free paper.

Acquisitions Editor: Carrie Brandon

Editorial Assistant: Duncan Marchbank

Production Editor: Bennie Clark Allen

Copy Editor: Sarah J. Duffy

Typesetter: C&M Digitals (P) Ltd.

Proofreader: Talia Greenberg

Indexer: Wendy Allex

Cover Designer: Anupama Krishnan

Marketing Manager: Jennifer Jones

SUSTAINABLE FORESTRY INITIATIVE

Certified Sourcing

www.sfiprogram.org

SFI-01075

17 18 19 20 21 10 9 8 7 6 5 4 3 2 1

• Contents •

• Preface •

In the last few years, I've been noodling over some very difficult puzzles. Policy problems are getting harder. Policymakers' quest for solutions is becoming more elusive. More policy experts are producing more analysis than ever before, and they're becoming increasingly unhappy that, too often, no one really seems to be paying attention to their work. And the American public is ever angrier about a government that just doesn't seem able to solve their problems.

It's a sad potpourri of frustration. Policymakers want what the analysts have. Analysts want to give policymakers what they need. Too often, the demand doesn't match up with the supply. When the match isn't made, and since so many policy players know what they want—or think they already know what is best—they make decisions and implement programs without the benefit of knowledge that could help reduce mistakes and improve results. It's no wonder that the public gets even unhappier.

And into this stew comes a new opportunity—and challenge. From sources as different as social media and mega-computers are coming enormous stockpiles of undigested (but often digestible) information—*big data*, as it's come to be known. We have counts about neighborhood crimes and ratings of restaurants. We know who gets which diseases and where the holdups in airport security lines are. This information creates great potential for learning new things, if we can figure out how to manage it.

Finally, there are fascinating new tools that can bring information to life. Google can map which Halloween costume is most popular in which town. Spreadsheets can help sort big piles of data into useful categories. There's still a vast contribution to be made by traditional statistical tools, like multiple regression. But this combination of forces has opened many new doors.

That defines the central focus of this book: Can we go through the door together, policymaker and analyst, to decide and implement policies better for the sake of citizens? The book is dedicated to the proposition that we can do better by knowing better—by improving the connection between analysts and decision makers, between supply and demand for information, and by making that connection in new and very exciting ways.

In preparing this book, I'm indebted to my students and to those on the front lines of data in government. They've all proven terrific teachers. And I'm also grateful for the wonderful support this project has received from CQ Press/SAGE, including the press's director, Charisse Kiino, and associate director, Matthew Byrnie. I want to thank acquisitions editor Carrie Brandon, editorial assistant Duncan Marchbank, and production editor Bennie Clark Allen, who was unfailingly helpful in getting the project to the finish line. It was a great pleasure to have the chance to work yet again with copy editor Sarah J. Duffy, who helped smooth the edges of my prose.

Most of all, I want to thank my wife, Sue, whose instincts about what's right and how best to get there have helped shape this book. I'm so grateful, now as ever, for her support over the years.

Donald F. Kettl
February 2017

• Acknowledgments •

The author and SAGE Publishing gratefully acknowledge the following reviewers for their kind assistance:

Raymond Alvarez, *University of West Virginia*

John Brennan, *University of North Carolina*

Jeanne-Marie Col, *John Jay College of Criminal Justice*

Lee Fritschler, *George Mason University*

Hollie Russon Gilman, *Columbia University*

Myung Jin, *Virginia Commonwealth University*

Carol Nechemias, *Pennsylvania State University*

Ann Quinley, *Pomona College*

• About the Author •

Donald F. Kettl is professor and former dean in the School of Public Policy at the University of Maryland. He is also a nonresident senior fellow at the Volcker Alliance, the Partnership for Public Service, and the Brookings Institution.

Kettl is the author or editor of many books and monographs, including *The Politics of the Administrative Process* (7th ed., 2017), *Can Government Earn Our Trust?* (2017), *Escaping Jurassic Government: How to Recover America's Lost Commitment to Competence* (2016), *System under Stress: The Challenge to 21st Century Governance* (2014), *The Next Government of the United States: Why Our Institutions Fail Us and How to Fix Them* (2008), and *The Global Public Management Revolution* (2005). He has twice won the Louis Brownlow Book Award of the National Academy of Public Administration for the best book published in public administration. In 2008, Kettl won the American Political Science Association's John Gaus Award for a lifetime of exemplary scholarship in political science and public administration. He was awarded the Warner W. Stockberger Achievement Award of the International Public Management Association for Human Resources in 2007 for outstanding contributions in the field of public-sector personnel management.

He holds a PhD in political science from Yale University. Prior to his appointment at the University of Maryland, he taught at the University of Pennsylvania, Columbia University, the University of Virginia, Vanderbilt University, and the University of Wisconsin–Madison. He is a fellow of Phi Beta Kappa and the National Academy of Public Administration.

Kettl has consulted broadly for government organizations at all levels, in the United States and abroad. He has appeared frequently in national and international media, including National Public Radio, *Good Morning America, ABC World News Tonight, NBC Nightly News, CBS Evening News,* CNN's *Anderson Cooper 360* and *The Situation Room,* the Fox News Channel, the Huffington Post, Al Jazeera, as well as public television's *News Hour* and the BBC. He is a regular columnist for *Governing* magazine, which is read by state and local government officials around the country. He chaired two gubernatorial blue-ribbon commissions for the Wisconsin state government, one on campaign finance reform and the other on government structure and finance. Kettl is a co-shareholder of the Green Bay Packers, along with his wife, Sue.

Knowing Better

For all the battles we have about public policy, we can probably all agree on at least two things. First, we can do much better. From trust in government to confidence in its ability to perform, there's near-universal agreement that government just doesn't work as well as it should. Few Americans trust government to do the right thing. According to a 2015 Pew Research Center poll, just 19 percent of those surveyed trust government do what's right "just about always" or "most of the time." In 1958, that number was more than three times higher, at 73 percent.[1]

Second, one way to *do* better is to *know* better what to do. That's the core of education, which American publisher William Feather defined as "being able to differentiate between what you do know and what you don't. It's knowing where to go to find out what you need to know; and it's knowing how to use the information once you get it."[2] We spend a lot of money, devote years of time, and invest much of ourselves in pursuit of that goal. It's true for our individual lives, and we carry that belief over to our social lives as well. To borrow from the poet Maya Angelou, if we knew better, we'd do better. That's the core of many candidates' campaigns: they know better, they'll do better, and they'll serve us better. That, after all, was the cornerstone of Donald Trump's 2016 "Make America Great Again" campaign.

Knowing, however, turns out to be a lot harder than it looks. David Dunning, an experimental social psychologist, suggests (only partially in jest) that "we are all confident idiots."[3] As evidence, he points to a long-running gag on Jimmy Kimmel's late-night television show, where his camera crews ask people on the street their views on world events and well-known people. At Austin's South by Southwest, the crew asked one festival-goer about a band that didn't exist. Did "Contact Dermatitis" have what it takes to make it to the big time? The man said,

"Absolutely." The crew got similar replies when people on Hollywood Boulevard were quizzed about whether the 2014 movie *Godzilla* was insensitive to those who survived a giant lizard attack on Tokyo or whether Bill Clinton got enough credit for bringing the Korean War to an end.

The research that Dunning conducted with one of his students, Justin Kruger, found that incompetent people can't see how incompetent they are. None of us knows everything, so the Dunning-Kruger effect applies to all of us. And how do we react? Not by becoming disoriented or worried, Dunning concluded. "Instead," he wrote, "the incompetent are blessed with an inappropriate confidence, buoyed by *something* that feels to them like knowledge." We tend to double-down on what we *think* we know, since that turns out to be easier than having to confront gaps in our knowledge and then work hard to fill them. It turns out to be "easy to judge the idiocy of others," to fail to recognize the idiocy in ourselves, and to spot the misinformation that too often shapes our decisions.[4] (It's worth noting, by the way, that "idiot" comes from the ancient Greek, referring to something that pertains to oneself. The self-centeredness of "idiot" bears directly on the search for knowing better, since the more one looks to oneself for knowledge, the more likely incompetence is likely to result.)

This complicates two foundations of our problem with a third. When it comes to public policy, we don't think government does well. We think it can—and should—do better. We think we can do better by knowing more. But we think we know more than we do, often don't recognize what we don't know, and think that those who disagree with us are idiots. Of course, there's nothing new here. Benjamin Franklin wrote, "A learned blockhead is a greater blockhead than an ignorant one."[5] And, as Franklin is quoted as saying, "The doorstep to the temple of wisdom is a knowledge of our own ignorance."[6] It's hard to do better when we don't know what we don't know, when the gap doesn't cause us personal concern, and when we can write off others whose views are different because we're convinced they just don't know what we know. It's hard to escape idiocy. And, of course, none of us believes we are idiots to begin with—that's always someone else's problem.

The gap between what we know—and what we can agree that we know—and what we *need* to know is enormous. Two former directors of the U.S. Office of Management and Budget, one Republican (Jim Nussle) and one Democrat (Peter Orszag), contend that "based on our estimate, less than one dollar out of every hundred dollars the federal government spends is backed by even the most basic evidence."[7] A former senior White House adviser for President George W. Bush, Ron Haskins, joined with Greg Margolis to plead, "Show me the evidence," in their 2015 book.[8] Investing more in knowing more, for many policy folks, is the key to making government work better.

We seek to escape extremely stupid behavior founded on doing things that don't work. We need to do better to make our democracy work better. Almost everyone agrees we need that escape. We know it's a very hard road because, if it were easy, we would have done so a long time ago, especially given the decades of time and billions of dollars we've spent trying to do better policy analysis. Only rarely do people do stupid things on purpose, especially when it comes to making big, expensive decisions affecting many other people. So how can we better solve the core Maya Angelou problem: *knowing better to do better*?

In fact, the problem of figuring out what we know and then determining what to do about it is getting bigger, and the problem is growing faster than we can keep up with. We are awash in an accelerating supply of information, which we call the *big data* movement. Everything we do is generating data—our web browsers are capturing vast supplies of what we are searching for and what we might want to buy, hidden cameras on our campuses and office buildings are collecting information on who is driving and walking where, and our music and video streaming services know what we are listening to and watching. Government and private organizations are also collecting lots of information on everything from where we live and drive to how much pollution we produce and how many jobs we create. If there were data sniffers, they would show that every step we take during the day leaves behind unimaginable—and often unimagined—trails of data. All of this information generates huge piles of big data—collections of raw numbers and information that can be digested into insights that can improve our decisions. In some cases, we can use traditional statistics like means, medians, variances, and regressions to wrestle these data into meaning. But in far more cases, we need new and better tools, which can sometimes provide even better insights. Sometimes little bites of this mega-supply can provide far better evidence for improving the public policies that shape our lives. Making good sense of all the data we have around us is the goal of this little book.

Doing without Knowing (Everything)

Nussle and Orszag are both right and wrong in trying to wrestle with the problem of evidence. They are right because fundamental, scientifically based data inform relatively little of our public policy. But they are wrong in arguing that only 1 percent of what government does is backed by "even the most basic evidence." In fact, there's *some* evidence backing up almost *everything* government does, even the wrong things. It's just that the evidence isn't always right, decision makers don't always follow what we know, and their decisions certainly don't always lead us in the right direction.

Consider, for example, the war in Iraq. American and British leaders argued in 2003 that they needed to go to war against Iraqi leader Saddam Hussein because he was stockpiling weapons of mass destruction and was on the verge of using them. In fact, there were no weapons of mass destruction. An exhaustive inquiry by Sir John Chilcot in the United Kingdom produced a devastating report. He concluded that analysts who made the case for war had overstated the evidence "with a certainty that was not justified." The nations failed to understand the consequences of the invasion, especially for how to deal with Iraq after Saddam's departure. And, most pointedly, "the Government failed to achieve its stated objectives." Moreover, "policy on Iraq was made on the basis of flawed intelligence and assessments. They were not challenged, and they should have been." As a result, the alliance found itself in a position that, Sir John said, was "humiliating."[9]

What accounts for such problems, here and in countless other cases? There are three cascading challenges:

1. *We don't know everything—and we never can.* The human limits on looking, understanding, processing, and deciding mean that we can never know everything that matters, even about important things in which we focus our efforts. Some of that flows from fundamental human bounds in processing information. Some of it comes from the fact that not everyone involved in a big policy decision shares all that they know. Saddam was notorious for puffing about his capabilities and for enshrouding his decisions in fog. It was hard for British and American intelligence analysts to know what was true and what wasn't. Toward the end, Saddam told everyone he did not have stockpiles of weapons of mass destruction, but British and American intelligence analysts simply didn't believe him. They were wrong—not because they wanted to be but because they failed to look hard enough, to apply enough checks to their own judgments, and to recognize that this might actually be a rare case when Saddam was telling the truth.

2. *Some of what we know is wrong.* Some of the intelligence leading analysts to conclude that Iraq held weapons of mass destruction came from a source that described a device containing spherical glass devices. The devices, in fact, bore a striking similarity to chemical weapons that actors Nicholas Cage and Sean Connery set out to destroy in the 1996 movie *The Rock* before a general played by Ed Harris could launch the weapons against San Francisco.[10] The Chilcot report, however, noted that nerve gas isn't typically carried in glass spheres—they can easily break and hurt everyone, including the soldiers planning to use them. What the intelligence source reported seemed to track with the movie, and the movie seemed to add credibility to the source's reports, even though experts knew it couldn't be real.[11]

3. *We don't need evidence to make decisions.* Analysts who produce serious policy analysis contend that the world would be better if policymakers listened to them more often (it would) and that policymakers should do so (but very often they do not). Charles E. Lindblom and David K. Cohen explain why. Policy analysts, they argue, "greatly overestimate the amount and distinctiveness of the information and analysis they offer for social problem solving." Even more important, they point out, society can—and often does—rely on "ordinary knowledge" to make decisions—information that flows from experience and common sense. For most problems, "people will

always depend heavily on ordinary knowledge." It is always available, it always provides at least some answer to every question, and it is not always clear to policymakers what value sophisticated policy analysis adds.[12]

Policymakers, of course, are invariably convinced that they know best what will best help their constituents. After all, they won their jobs by putting their case to the people and winning elections. It's little surprise that this convinces them that they have a good sense of the pulse of the voters—better, certainly, than analysts who have never had to run for office. Nothing better reinforces their sense of the power of ordinary knowledge than standing in front of thousands of cheering fans and then winning more votes than anyone running against them. That makes it easy for them to become convinced that they have all the insight they need to govern well.

The Law of Supply and Demand

These challenges lead to a central fact: no matter how much evidence analysts slide before government's policymakers and managers, policymakers won't use it unless it is useful to them. It is one thing to make the case for a larger, more powerful supply of evidence, as Nussle and Orszag have done. But it's quite another to create a larger *demand* by policymakers for evidence. Unless government's policy people want it and use it, producing more of it will not affect policy one bit. Policy people will only seek evidence that helps them solve problems they need or want to solve.

There's an understandable dilemma at the core of much analysis about government. Analysts look at government's performance and know it can be better—and they're right. They believe that knowing better can make it better—and they're right. They believe that they can study problems better, learn more, provide evidence, and move policy in a stronger direction—but too often they're frustrated. Analysts' answers aren't always the ones that top policy officials find easy to accept. In fact, the answers aren't always to questions that these officials want answered. Sometimes there's a mismatch between the analysts' work and policymakers' questions because analysts, driven by the techniques they've worked so hard to hone, go where the data are. Sometimes they focus on the issues that they think are most important and would benefit most from their work. Sometimes they don't have enough contact with policymakers to know what problems most need analysis. Sometimes they don't provide answers in a form that policymakers find digestible. For a variety of reasons, analysts who focus on supplying analysis often end up discouraged by the gap between the things they say and the actions that policy officials take. That's the supply-side problem.

Then there's the demand-side problem. Policy officials sometimes have little patience for the rigor and arcane methods of policy analysis. Sophisticated statistical techniques, like multiple regression and analysis of variance, often speak in a language that policymakers can't translate. Policy officials complain that the focus on uncertainty and significance tests clouds the meaning of the data—and confounds their need to make black-or-white, up-or-down decisions. They point to the fact that much of the data and analysis is backward-looking, based on what analysts could study about programs in the past and based on data already at hand, while they need to make decisions about the future. While they might not say it, they often trust their own instincts more than the studies that analysts present. In a nutshell, they sometimes think that analyses don't answer the problems they face in ways that help them solve them.

That produces a gap between the supply side and demand side of analysis. Suppliers of evidence often don't give policy officials what they need, when they need it, in a form they can use, on the problems where they need the most help. Users, on the demand side, often don't find the evidence useful. We unfortunately often end up, as a result, spending a lot of time producing evidence that policy officials don't use; policy officials spend a lot of their time making mistakes that better evidence could help them avoid. We can do better if we know better. We can know better about what works. But, too often, there's a gap between the knowing and the doing. And that isn't good for anyone.

Making Evidence Speak

Making policy better—escaping the kind of idiocy that Dunning described—requires closing the supply-demand gap in public policy evidence. We need to find a balance between the evidence that analysts supply (or want to) and the evidence that policymakers demand (or can be convinced to). That leads to the five principles:

> Principle 1: *Evidence is of no use to anyone unless its consumers want it and use it.* That requires producing the supply of the evidence that decision makers want and need. It also requires creating demand from decision makers for evidence that will prove useful. This is the challenge of balancing supply and demand.

> Principle 2: *It's important to get the story, and get it right.* Evidence comes in a wide variety of forms, from the "gold standard" of policy analysis, randomized controlled trials, to impressions picked up off the streets. Good evidence is valid, reliable, and timely. This is the challenge of data analytics.

> Principle 3: *It's important to tell the story in ways that capture what the evidence says (and thus fits what analysts who supply it know) and in language that will be clear (and thus fits what policymakers who demand it need to know).* This is the challenge of data visualization.

> Principle 4: *It's important to sell the story in ways that make the evidence convincing.* Analysts sometimes assume that, after they've worked through the vast complexities of the problems they're studying, their results will speak for

themselves. They never do, both because there's always uncertainty around the findings and because many other voices are competing for the decision makers' ears. This is the challenge of policy persuasion.

Principle 5: *It's important that the evidence speak above the noise.* We are increasingly living in a world in which there is boundless information, always swirling in a news cycle that never ends. Knowing better requires putting careful analysis, some of which takes years to develop, into a turbulent environment where, in minutes, social media can transform everything, including what analysts sometimes have struggled for years to study and learn. To do better, we need to know better, and knowing better requires solving this last challenge: immediate transparency.

These are the challenges in the world of public policy that we face in *knowing*. We'll explore strategies for solving these challenges in the coming chapters, beginning with challenge two: working through the many streams of policy-relevant data.

Notes

1. Pew Research Center, "Beyond How Americans View Their Government" (November 23, 2015), http://www.people-press .org/2015/11/23/1-trust-in-government-1958-2015. Small portions of the argument in this chapter originally appeared in two pieces I've written: "Making Data Speak: Lessons for Using Numbers for Solving Public Policy Puzzles," *Governance* 29 (2016), 573–579; and *Escaping Jurassic Government: How to Recover America's Lost Commitment to Competence* (Washington, D.C.: Brookings Institution, 2016).

2. "William Feather," Wikiquote, https://en.wikiquote.org/wiki/ William_Feather.

3. David Dunning, "We Are All Confident Idiots," *Pacific Standard* (October 27, 2014), https://psmag.com/we-are-all-confident-idiots-56a60eb7febc# .4hnv1jdnh; see also David Dunning and Justin Kruger, "Unskilled and Unaware of It: How Difficulties in Recognizing One's Own Incompetence Lead to Inflated Self-Assessments," *Journal of Personality and Social Psychology* 77 (1999), 1121–1134.

4. Ibid.

5. "A Learned Blockhead Is a Greater Blockhead than an Ignorant One," Founders' Quotes, http://foundersquotes .com/founding-fathers-quote/a-learned-blockhead-is-a-greater-blockhead-than-an-ignorant-one.

6. "Benjamin Franklin Quotes," Brainy Quote, http://www.brainy quote.com/quotes/quotes/b/ benjaminfr163094.html.

7. Jim Nussle and Peter Orszag, "Let's Play Moneyball," in *Moneyball for Government*, ed. Jim Nussle and Peter Orszag (Washington, D.C.: Disruption Books, 2014), 4.

8. Ron Haskins and Greg Margolis, *Show Me the Evidence: Obama's Fight for Rigor and Results in Social Policy* (Washington, D.C.: Brookings Institution, 2015).

9. "Statement by Sir John Chilcot: 6 July 2016," in *The Iraq Inquiry*, pp. 2, 6, 11, http://www.iraqin quiry.org.uk/media/247010/ 2016-09-06-sir-john-chilcots- public-statement.pdf.

10. Kim Sengupta, "Chilcot Report: MI6 May Have Got Crucial Intelligence on Iraq WMDs from a Nicolas Cage Film," *Independent* (July 7, 2016), http://www .independent.co.uk/news/uk/ politics/chilcot-report-iraq-war- inquiry-wmds-mi6-evidence- tony-blair-richard-dearlove- a7124426.html.

11. *The Iraq Inquiry*, Section 4.3, p. 313, http://www.iraqinquiry.org.uk/ media/246496/the-report-of-the- iraq-inquiry_section-43 .pdf#search=movie.

12. Charles E. Lindblom and David K. Cohen, *Usable Knowledge: Social Science and Social Problem Solving* (New Haven: Yale University Press, 1979), 12.

Get the Story, Get It Right

I f we want to do better, we need to know better. And knowing better begins with knowing what problems we most need to solve.

What Are the Right Questions?

Policymakers face an endless stream of decisions, and even more boundless swells of information. Few government programs are simple. Government's managers can't drive within narrow lanes to solve any of their important problems. Navigating this world is exceptionally complex, and doing better requires better answers to the right questions. There are five fundamental questions for which policymakers need good answers:[1]

1. *Hindsight.* What does the past teach us about the future?

2. *Foresight.* How can we make good decisions to produce the best results?

3. *Results.* What have we accomplished—and how can we do better?

4. *Risk.* What challenges do we face that could undermine what we want to do?

5. *Resilience.* How can we bounce back when, inevitably, bad things happen?

Let's look at each of these five questions—and the kinds of evidence that can help us answer them so we can learn better.

Hindsight

One of the best ways to know the best answer to the problems we face is to learn lessons from what's happened before. Evidence from programs in the past can provide powerful clues about the best decisions for the future.

Program evaluation is the tool for doing this.[2] It systematically looks at how public programs have worked in the past, what results they produced, and how well the results matched the goals policymakers intended. In Rialto, California, for example, the police department equipped its officers with cameras. The result: the number of complaints against officers dropped by 88 percent in a twelve-month period, and officers' use of force went down by 60 percent. The police chief concluded that the cameras were the cause.[3]

The evidence certainly seems strong. But how could the department know for sure that it was the use of cameras that drove the numbers down? All of the officers began wearing cameras. Without a control group of officers without cameras but working the same duty, careful analysts would point out, it would be very hard to know the precise cause.

That's why researchers hold *randomized controlled trials* (RCTs) as the gold standard for evidence. In these studies, analysts follow the basic approach of medical researchers. They assess a program's results by randomly assigning those taking part in the program into two groups: one group receives the program's treatment (whether it's a job training program or a different way of running probation), and another group is as identical as possible—except it doesn't receive the program's treatment. Analysts examine the results to determine whether those who get the treatment (the experimental group) get better results than those who don't (in the control group). Random assignment helps control for differences in results that could be explained by *who* takes part in a program; for example, if released prisoners with the best education volunteer for a new probation program, they might have an easier time staying out of jail because their education might help them get better jobs.

But, of course, it's often hard to randomly assign individuals to programs. It can be hard to treat different individuals in the same neighborhood differently (for example, in experimenting with different strategies for garbage pickup). It can be hard to deny treatment to some individuals for the purpose of creating control groups (for example, when a dangerous disease breaks out and experts think they have a vaccine that could save victims). It can be expensive to do RCTs, the results take time to develop, and policymakers are often eager to press ahead with programs they deeply believe in. Imagine a policymaker saying publicly, "I have a great idea for a program. I'm going to spend a lot of money on it. I really think it's going to work. But half of you can't get it because you're in the control group." There are strategies to resolve this challenge, but developing the very best research tools can often prove quite difficult in the very real world of politics.

One of the highest hurdles to jump in sharpening our hindsight is simple: policymakers are often attracted to ideas, and once they sink their teeth into them, it's often hard to let go. A premier example is the "Scared Straight" program, which grew out of the efforts in the 1970s to reduce juvenile crime. Kids who get picked up for offenses are sent for a day to adult prisons, where they get the full "in your face" treatment from prisoners, guards, and counselors. There's everything from prison chow and inmates screaming to threats of violence and the chance to wear prison uniforms for the day. "If you keep on your path," the program suggests, "here's the life you can expect to live." Policymakers have loved the program for decades—and so, too, has television. It started with a 1978 documentary, which won an Academy Award. Sequels followed, as did a long-running television series on the A&E cable network, starting in 2011. *Beyond Scared Straight* was a ratings winner for the network, and the Spike network picked up reruns. It was engaging television. And policymakers were hooked. Didn't it make sense that exposing kids to prison would make them want to do everything they could to avoid it in the future?

Researchers took a careful look at this program and concluded that it had a big impact. "Scared Straight" actually *increased* crime among the kids who went through the program. As Assistant Attorney General for the Office of Criminal Justice Programs Laurie O. Robinson and the Office of Juvenile Justice and Delinquency Prevention's acting administrator, Jeff Slowikowski, put it in 2011, "'Scared straight' is not only ineffective but is potentially harmful."[4] How could they be so sure? A team of researchers led by Anthony Petrosino, Carolyn Turpin Petrosino, and John Buehler explored randomized controlled trials on the program and concluded, "Simply put, participating in the program was *associated with an increase in crime.*"[5] Some of the evidence is shaky. Other studies produce solid conclusions. But the overall picture is clear: "Scared Straight" is an effective program—for increasing crime (see Table 2.1).

That hasn't stopped policymakers or worried parents. One Georgia parent said, "I tried to do everything I could do as a parent," before sending her sons to the local sheriff's office for a "scared straight" experience. The television show continued to convince parents, especially desperate ones, that the program might give their kids a chance. "It's a strong thing in America that we believe that being tough on people, punishing people, coercing them—basically forcing them to behave the way we want them to behave—it will somehow work," explained Jeffrey Butts, a criminology expert at John Jay College. "We get a lot of folks that will bring their kids by and say kind of the same thing," one senior official in Georgia's Richmond County Sherriff's Office explained. "They'll say 'I can't make this kid do anything, you guys need to scare them.'" So scare them they do—even though the evidence says that the results are likely to be more kids committing more crimes.[6] Knowing better doesn't necessarily always lead to doing better, even when the knowing comes from the gold standard of policy research.

TABLE 2.1 • Evidence on the Effectiveness of "Scared Straight"

Program	Number of participants	Results	Other information
Michigan (1967)	60	43 percent of program group committed another crime versus 17 percent of control group	Report is brief, with few details
Illinois (1979)	161	17 percent of program group had new contacts with police versus 12 percent of control group	Results not statistically significant, but outcomes negative
Michigan JOLT Program (1979)	227	Little difference between program group and control group	
Virginia Insiders Program (1981)	80	At six months: 41 percent of program group back in court versus 39 percent of control group, but results not statistically significant	Little difference between the two groups, but large dropout rate for program: 55 percent at 12 months
Texas Face-to-Face Program (1981)	160	After six months: control group outperformed each of three treatment groups assigned to prison orientation and/or counseling. Delinquency rates: • Control: 28 percent • Orientation, counseling: 39 percent • Orientation only: 36 percent • Counseling only: 39 percent	None of the findings are statistically significant

Program	Number of participants	Results	Other information
New Jersey "Scared Straight" Program (1982)	82	After six months: 11 percent of control group committed new crimes versus 41 percent of program group	Difference statistically significant
California SQUIRES Program (1983)	108	After 12 months: 67 percent of control group rearrested versus 81 percent of program group	Program participants rearrested stayed out of the system a bit longer: 4.1 months versus 3.3 months for control group
Kansas Juvenile Education Program (1986)	52	No difference	
Mississippi Project Aware (1992)	176	Little difference at 12 and 24 months	

Source: Adapted from Anthony Petrosino, Carolyn Turpin Petrosino, and John Buehler, *"Scared Straight" and Other Juvenile Awareness Programs for Preventing Juvenile Delinquency* (Oslo, Norway: Campbell Systematic Reviews, 2004), https://www.campbellcollaboration.org/media/k2/attachments/Scared_Straight_R.pdf.

Foresight

Analysts also try to help policymakers through forecasts about the future. They build complex models, based on past data, to predict the future. Nowhere is this more important than in economic policy. The growth of the economy not only is important in its own right. It also powerfully shapes government spending. Lower economic growth tends to drive spending up (because more citizens get government benefits) and revenues down (because there is less income to tax and money to spend). Forecasting the budget—especially the size of the federal deficit—thus depends heavily on the foresight of the forecasters.

But how accurate are these forecasts? In dealing with the federal budget, there are two major government teams: one working for the president, in the Office of Management and Budget (OMB), and the other working for Congress, in the Congressional Budget Office (CBO). These are some of the best economic forecasters in the world. They do very well—but they don't always get their forecasts right. Of course, it's a mistake to frame the issue that way. *Nobody* gets these complicated issues right all the time. Rather, there are three questions that matter most. First, do the forecasters get it mostly right, most of the time? Second, are some forecasters better than others? And third, when they get it wrong, what difference does it make?

It's possible to answer the first two questions together. OMB and CBO almost always come within just 2 percent of the actual economic growth. Most of the time they're within 1 percent. In an economy as large and complex as the United States, and with as many global forces pushing on the economy, that's remarkable. Moreover, as Figure 2.1 shows, one tends to do about as well as the other—and, for that matter, they do about as well as the very best private-sector forecasters. When they miss, they tend to miss at about the same level in about the same direction.

What difference do the errors make? Most of the time, not much—and the errors tend to even out over time. But at the beginning of Barack Obama's presidency, as the figure shows, all the forecasters—government as well as private—missed their forecasts of economic growth by large margins. All of them forecast that the 2008 economic downturn would be much less severe than it turned out to be. Obama used those forecasts to make his plans. He miscalculated in those plans because the forecasters miscalculated in their forecasts.

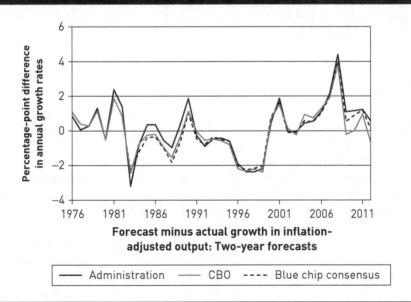

FIGURE 2.1 • Accuracy in Forecasting: Forecast Economic Growth Minus Actual Growth

Forecast minus actual growth in inflation-adjusted output: Two-year forecasts

—— Administration   —— CBO   ---- Blue chip consensus

Source: "Growth in Inflation-Adjusted Output: Two-Year Forecasts." Congressional Budget Office, *CBO's Economic Forecasting Record: 2015 Update* (February 12, 2015), https://www.cbo.gov/publication/49891.

That had a huge impact on the first years of the Obama administration. On taking office in January 2009, the president had a clear strategy.[7] The economy was in free fall, so he would take his lumps early and then move out briskly with new policy plans as the economy recovered. The recession, his administration believed, would be nasty but short. The plan was to pump money out fast, through a stimulus program, and then follow quickly with the administration's policy agenda, especially health-care reform. It smelled like a good plan, especially since it would help Obama regain momentum going into the 2012 presidential campaign, and his advisers believed that the economic forecasts would support the effort. The forecasters got the first part of the equation right. The recession was nasty. But the recovery was painfully slow. That led to the "jobless recovery," as analysts christened it, and it plagued Obama well into his second term.

But this wasn't a forecasting error by just the president's own economists. Nearly everyone missed the jobless recovery. In early 2009, the Office of Management and Budget projected an unemployment rate for the year at 8.1 percent. The nonpartisan Congressional Budget Office's forecast was a bit higher, at 8.3 percent. Private economists didn't do much better. The top fifty-five forecasters surveyed by the *Wall Street Journal* were even more optimistic—they thought unemployment would be 8.5 percent. In fact, unemployment for the year was 9.9 percent. The longer-term forecasts also missed the mark. In early 2009, OMB estimated that unemployment would drop to 5.6 percent by 2012. CBO was more bearish, with an estimate of 6.8 percent. But both forecasts were well short of the actual unemployment rate of 7.9 percent (see Figure 2.2).

And how did they miss it? CBO's own analysis is instructive.[8] A quarter of the error came from a downturn that turned out to be even nastier than expected—but two-thirds came from a "reassessment of trends": CBO, along with most forecasters, just didn't see the emergence of the post-recession "new normal," with relatively slow economic growth and even slower job creation. The world had changed, at least for the medium term, and most of the forecasters didn't see it coming.

The computers didn't tell the forecasters that the world had changed. And the errors helped cook Obama's political goose before he was even sworn in. If the consensus economic forecasts had panned out, he would have been able to campaign for reelection in 2012 as a second Franklin D. Roosevelt who turned the nasty downturn around. Democrats running in 2014 would have been talking to a much happier electorate. He would have had a much more open field for policy initiatives instead of having the jobless recovery hanging around his political neck. At least for a while, the conventional wisdom was that Obama had lost his political mojo. This constellation of forces fueled the Republicans' takeover of Congress in 2014, and it set the stage for the epic fight for the middle class that helped shaped the 2016 presidential election. Hillary Clinton would have been able to connect with happy voters, and Donald Trump would not have had large, angry legions to tap into. All this flowed from how most private and public economists missed the call in late 2008.

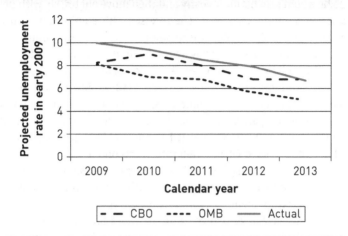

FIGURE 2.2 • Unemployment Forecasts by OMB and CBO

Sources: Office of Management and Budget, *Budget of the United States Government: Analytical Perspectives— Fiscal Year 2010* (2009); Congressional Budget Office, *Budget and Economic Outlook: 2009–2019* (February 2009); Bureau of Labor Statistics, *Labor Force Statistics from the Current Population Survey* (Washington, D.C.: U.S. Department of Labor).

Note: Spring 2009 forecasts for unemployment for each of the next five calendar years, compared with actual unemployment.

We struggle to get foresight into what's going to happen. A lot of the time, we do pretty well. But sometimes the models fall short, and when this happens, the results can be large and devastating.

Results

Taking long looks back and making long predictions into the future aren't enough for policymakers. They need to be constantly alert to what's happening with the programs they run: to see trends as they are emerging, detect problems creeping into the system, find opportunities to do things better, and strengthen the implementation of government programs. This is the broad area of *performance management:* monitoring the operation of programs through sophisticated measures, in as close to real time as possible, and using that information to improve operations.[9]

For example, cities ranging from Louisville to Chicago have put restaurant inspection data online, so diners can see whether the spots where they eat are safe. The *New York Times* website has displayed a map showing the grades that restaurants received in their last inspection, and the inspection grades must be posted in the window of the restaurant, so diners know the safety of the establishment before they walk through the door. For example, it's possible to search on the map of central Manhattan and find all the restaurants with a grade of C on the city's

A-B-C scale (with A being the highest; see Figure 2.3). The evidence not only helps consumers. It also helps the city target its inspection efforts. At the federal Centers for Disease Control and Prevention, the PulseNet system allows the agency to track the outbreak of food-borne illnesses so it has an early warning of emerging problems—and can respond quickly.[10]

This strategy came from a dinner in a swank New York restaurant on a winter night in 1994. A seasoned New York City transit cop, Jack Maple, sketched out a plan—on a napkin—to revolutionize the city's crime-fighting. Four principles, he said, could drive improvements:

1. Accurate and timely intelligence

2. Rapid deployment

3. Effective tactics

4. Relentless follow-up and assessment

The plan, christened CompStat, was data-driven at its core. The "accurate and timely intelligence" shifted the NYPD to compiling long lists of crimes to place-specific maps, which plotted crimes as they happened instead of on reports months later. It moved the system from pins on a wall to sophisticated computer-based mapping. And in 2016 it took an additional step, with a new generation of reporting, which allowed the NYPD to track crimes block by block and to report up-to-date crime rates on the city's website so its planners—and all citizens—could see the data (see Figure 2.4). CompStat, in turn, drove a vast revolution in improving the implementation of public programs by mapping what's happening, and doing it in real time. It was based on the premise that better policy was nothing without better results—and that the backbone of producing better results was knowing more, faster, about what was happening.

Results, after all, are what matter most. So the key lies in being able to track them—in real time and in a clear picture.

Risk

In August 2016, Michigan officials arraigned Liane Shekter Smith, the official formerly in charge of drinking water for the Michigan Department of Environmental Quality (MDEQ), for "willful neglect of duty." Between April 2014 and October 2015, complaints mounted about water in Flint. In February 2016, the state fired her for poor performance. Governor Rich Snyder, without referring to Smith by name, said that "some DEQ actions lacked common sense and that resulted in this terrible tragedy in Flint." Six months later, an investigator told the court that Smith had "intentionally misled and took affirmative steps to conceal from her supervisors at the MDEQ and the public the safety and severe health risk associated with using the water."[11]

FIGURE 2.3 • New York Restaurants with a Grade of C

Source: Jeremy White, "New York Health Department Restaurant Ratings Map," *New York Times* (screenshot on August 5, 2016), http://www.nytimes.com/interactive/dining/new-york-health-department-restaurant-ratings-map.html?_r=0.

FIGURE 2.4 • New York City Crime Map

Source: New York City Police Department. Map is for the month of July 2016. The darker the color, the higher the crime rate in the neighborhood. See https://maps.nyc.gov/crime.

In April 2014, Flint switched from getting its water from the Detroit Water and Sewerage Department to the Flint River. Almost immediately, some residents began complaining that the water had a bad taste. At first, state and local officials argued that the water was safe. It took months for investigators to conclude that the water, in fact, had high levels of lead, which entered the bloodstreams of some of the city's children. Lead has been found to cause behavioral and health problems in children, and there's no known treatment. In Flint, 40.1 percent of the water sampled in 272 homes had lead at 5 parts per billion (ppb). Ten percent of the homes had levels of 25 ppb, well above the U.S. Environmental Protection Agency's 15 ppb limit that requires an intervention. Some homes were higher than 100 ppb— and in one home, the level was astronomical: more than 1,000 ppb, according to a study undertaken by Virginia Tech scientists, who helped break the story.[12]

The average lead level was 10.6 ppb, but one of every eight homes had lead above the EPA's standard of 15 ppb. Figure 2.5 shows the distribution of the homes in the study by quintile (that is, broken down in 20 percent ranges, with the lowest quintile being the first 20 percent of the homes in the sample and the highest quintile being the last 20 percent of the homes). The top quintile of homes, on average, had lead levels of 38.4 ppb, more than twice the EPA's limit. This was, to put it simply, a huge public health crisis.

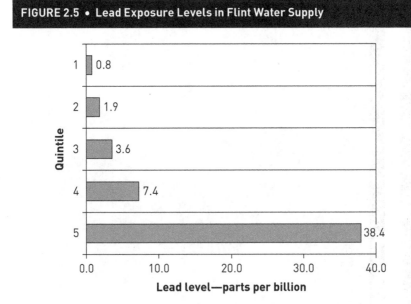

FIGURE 2.5 • Lead Exposure Levels in Flint Water Supply

Source: "[Complete Dataset] Lead Results from Tap Water Sampling in Flint, MI," Flint Water Study (December 1, 2015), http://flintwaterstudy.org/2015/12/complete-dataset-lead-results-in-tap-water-for-271-flint-samples.

It was a tragedy that so many children had been exposed to such high levels of lead. This was a problem that they would have to deal with for the rest of their lives. But it was a tragedy that could have been foreseen, since lead exposure in drinking water is a known issue. The EPA has set lead and copper limits in drinking water since 1991. If lead in the drinking water exceeds the 15 ppb level in more than 10 percent of the water taps, federal regulations require water suppliers to take action. In Flint, the number was 16 percent. Experts later concluded that the problem could have been completely prevented had the community used corrosion controls in the new system. An engineering professor at the University of Michigan, Glenn Daigger, said, "That is absolutely something that should be provided."[13]

The result was a huge problem. Children had been exposed to lead in their drinking water. State officials looked the other way as evidence about the problem mounted. Scientists plaintively called for action as their tests showed high levels of lead. Installing the corrosion prevention system in advance would have prevented the problem. Experts in the field have long known about the risks of lead in drinking water, and they've known that corrosion protection systems can effectively treat it. But the state and local officials decided not to install such a system.

In short, this was a failure of risk management: the process by which experts assess a decision, in advance, to determine what problems might result from the decision. Sometimes risks are obvious only after they occur.[14] But anticipating risk is very often possible. So, too, is avoiding it—or, at least, reducing the costs of problems when they occur. Experts point to six steps:

1. *Get the leaders on board,* since nothing can happen at all unless the top officials are committed to looking down the road and preventing problems before they happen.

2. *Identify risks,* especially by establishing a culture inside the agency to look for risks instead of trying to duck potential problems for fear of criticism.

3. *Assess risks,* particularly by building an understanding of what causes the risks and what the organization needs—in budgets, information technology, expertise, and other resources—to attack them.

4. *Develop an action plan* by creating a response to risks that fits the organization's mission and culture.

5. *Monitor risks* so that organizations and their leaders are not surprised and so they can detect and prevent problems while they are still small and more manageable.

6. *Communicate about risks,* to both elected officials and citizens, so that more transparency into operations increases confidence that the organization can tackle the problems it faces.[15]

In Flint, officials did not work thoroughly to identify risks in advance. When evidence began to surface about lead in the drinking water, they first ignored it, then were not sure whether to believe it. Only when outside investigators produced proof did they begin communicating about the risks and begin to act—and by then it was too late. Children had absorbed lead into their bodies and it will not go away. In contrast, the U.S. Transportation Security Administration has an aggressive risk–management system that focuses on identifying the full range of risks that could get in the way of its ability to protect flyers when they board airplanes. The National Institute of Standards and Technology even surveyed its top executives to determine their appetite for risk, which helped the organization determine how much risk it was likely to be able to take on—and where a somewhat lower appetite for risk among top managers made it harder for the organization to innovate fast enough to stay ahead of tough, complex technology issues. Working hard in advance to identify risk—and then equipping the organization to deal with it and staying ahead of a quickly changing world—can help government organizations perform much better. It can also help avoid actions like the ones that crippled Flint's water system.

Resilience

An important part of knowing is learning how to bounce back when things go wrong—and try as we might, they inevitably do. No one intended for government at all levels to stagger in responding to Hurricane Katrina in 2005, and the Obama administration surely never intended for its flagship health-care program, the Affordable Care Act, to fall flat on its face at its launch in 2013.[16] But smart policymakers know that, try as hard as they might to answer the first four questions, it is hard to escape the fifth: What to do when things go wrong?[17]

No one wants to imagine that failure can occur, let alone plan for it. NASA's long-term flight director Gene Kranz, in fact, wrote a book titled *Failure Is Not an Option*.[18] The movie *Apollo 13* made Kranz and his slogan famous, as NASA worked furiously to bring back the crew flying in a badly damaged spacecraft. But smart policymakers know that no program completely succeeds in fulfilling everything we want it to do and that failure is often not only an option—it sometimes is inescapable. Some of that, especially in public programs, is because our ambition leads us to reach far (sometimes too far). Some of that is because we can never completely answer these questions. Foresight is surely never perfect, and hindsight is only 20–20 when it's too late. It's hard to know what results we're producing or what risks we're taking. When the first four questions fail, policymakers must turn to *resilience*. As Judith Rodin explains in her book *The Resilience Dividend: Being Strong in a World Where Things Go Wrong*, "Resilience is the capacity of any entity—an individual, a community, an organization, or a natural system—to prepare for disruptions, to recover from shocks and stresses, and to adapt and grow from a disruptive experience." And the stronger an entity's resilience, the better it's able to bounce back when bad things happen. That, she says, is the "resilience dividend."[19]

Resilience is a tough challenge to attack. Big problems often bring big risks, and when they lead to failures they cause even larger recriminations ("How could you have allowed that to happen?" and "Why weren't you smart enough to see this coming?"). Spending money in advance, like fortifying the levees in New Orleans to prevent massive flooding after Hurricane Katrina's onslaught in 2005, can seem like a waste if there's no imminent crisis. Building political support to look far down the road, to tackle little problems before they become big ones, can be hard for politicians whose vision stretches only to the next election. (This is a spinoff of the economists' notion of discounting: citizens value benefits now more than benefits down the road.) But there's one inescapable fact: it's almost always cheaper to spend a little money in advance to help avoid or mitigate problems, than to clean them up after they explode. For instance, the Global Resilience Partnership concluded that 47 percent of all weather-related disasters are due to flooding alone.[20] It's impossible to stop all floods, but careful planning of projects like dams, drainage, and levees can go a long way toward reducing the damage when big storms occur.

For example, in 2004, just a year before Katrina savaged New Orleans, the Federal Emergency Management Agency ran a simulation of the impact of a big storm, christened "Hurricane Pam" for the exercise, on the region. The exercise predicted that such a storm would push water over the levees and submerge much of New Orleans.[21] For example, after Hurricane Katrina's devastating assault on New Orleans in 2005, the Federal Emergency Management Agency did a careful review of the areas of the city most at risk for flooding in another storm. The result was a new set of maps, produced in 2016, which highlighted the neighborhoods that could find themselves under water in a fierce storm— and where homeowners would be required to buy flood insurance (see Figure 2.6). But this new review also raised big questions for some New Orleans residents, because FEMA removed many neighborhoods from the flood plain. New flood control systems built after Katrina offered residents much more protection, and FEMA took them into account in drawing the maps. That was good news for the city, which was working hard to lure home buyers back into areas that Katrina had devastated, and many developers had lobbied hard to shrink the flood plain. Analysts warned, however, that the shrunken flood zone didn't necessarily mean that homeowners should drop their insurance. Another Katrina-sized storm could damage their homes yet again and, without insurance, they could face devastating losses. Resilience means planning for risks and taking the best actions to minimize their costs, on questions where there seldom are black-and-white answers. In a city like New Orleans, however, where so much of the land is near or below sea level, deciding where to draw the line is a difficult and contentious decision.

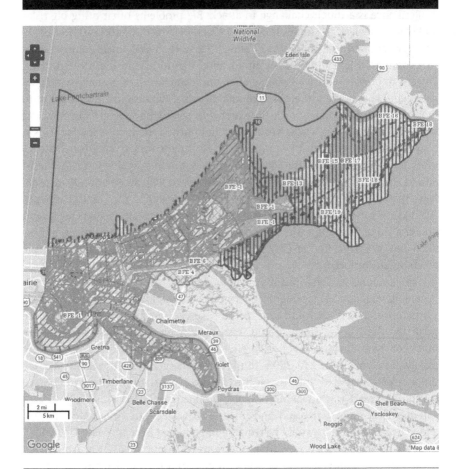

FIGURE 2.6 • FEMA Flood Information Portal Risk Map of New Orleans

Source: Federal Emergency Management Agency.

It's not easy, either politically or economically, to plan for resilience. But the tale of Katrina shows that we often know enough to do better—and that doing better sooner is a lot cheaper than trying to catch up after disasters strike. It's just hard to build the case, both politically and budgetarily, to do what needs to be done.

What Is a Good Answer?

We started this chapter by asking: What are the right questions? There are five: hindsight, foresight, results, risk, and resilience. But as we explore them, what are good answers? As we'll see in the chapters that follow, good answers not only help us with these five issues. They also help us deal with three big, overarching puzzles:

- *Silos of information.* The key to effective problem solving, as we've seen in this chapter, is information. But too often, the information we have is trapped in "silos of information," as G. Edward Deseve puts it—evidence generated within individual agencies and programs and that often fails to connect with larger problems.[22] No problem that matters any longer fits inside any one agency or program.[23] If we're going to find good answers, we need information that isn't trapped in agency or programmatic silos. We'll explore how to help evidence escape and drive good decisions.

- *Provide convincing answers to important questions.* In part, this is a problem of doing good research that meets the standards of careful analysis. Randomized controlled trials, for example, provide a guide for how to assess which results are real. So, too, do the significance tests that accompany data analysis. But, more broadly, we need evidence that is convincing, that provides solid answers to the questions that policymakers are asking—or need to ask—in ways that give them confidence to move forward. We've built the foundation for attacking the problem in this chapter, and we'll explore it in more detail in the chapters to come.

- *Deal with values.* In the end, answering each of these five big questions means sorting out the values that policymakers—and citizens—believe in. Evidence can help shape these values. Values, on the other hand, are often the prism through which policymakers look at evidence. One of the most important contributions that good evidence makes is to bring greater power and transparency to this fundamental puzzle. What values are we trying to advance with the policy decisions we make? How well are we doing to advance those values? Are there things we could do to improve our results?

Greater transparency through better evidence can help us attack these questions better. It can, of course, also heighten political tensions by shining a bright light on value conflicts that otherwise might have more comfortably stayed hidden below the surface. Sometimes policymakers don't really *want* to know the answer to these questions because the answers can force them to resolve more difficult problems. But as trust in government plummets and budgetary resources get tighter, burying tough problems only tends to make the big challenges worse. And with a bit of skill and some occasional luck, knowing better can help everyone involved work through these tough questions. In the next chapter, we'll explore how *telling the story* can help contribute to this process.

Notes

1. For an exploration of several of these questions, see G. Edward Deseve, *Enhancing the Government's Decision-Making: Helping Leaders Make Smart and Timely Decisions* (Washington, DC: Partnership for Public Service, 2016), http://www .businessofgovernment.org/sites/ default/files/Enhancing%20 the%20Government's%20 Decision-Making_0.pdf.

2. See, for example, Kathryn E. Newcomer, Harry P. Hatry, and Joseph S. Wholey, *Handbook of Practical Program Evaluation*, 4th ed. (San Francisco: Jossey-Bass, 2015).

3. Ian Lovett, "In California, a Champion for Police Cameras," *New York Times* (August 21, 2013), http://www.nytimes.com/ 2013/08/22/us/in-california-a- champion-for-police-cameras .html?smprod=nytcore-ipad& smid=nytcore-ipad-share.

4. Laurie O. Robinson and Jeff Slowikowski, "Scary—and Ineffective: Traumatizing at-Risk Kids Is Not the Way to Lead Them away from Crime and Drugs," *Baltimore Sun* (January 31, 2011), http://articles.baltimoresun .com/2011-01-31/news/bs-ed- scared-straight-20110131_1_ straight-type-programs-straight- program-youths.

5. Anthony Petrosino, Carolyn Turpin Petrosino, and John Buehler, *"Scared Straight" and Other Juvenile Awareness Programs for Preventing Juvenile Delinquency* (Oslo, Norway: Campbell Systematic Reviews, 2004), 34, https://www.campbell collaboration.org/media/ k2/attachments/Scared_ Straight_R.pdf.

6. Elly Yu, "At 'Wit's End': Scared Straight Programs Remain Popular among Parents Despite Warnings," *Juvenile Justice Information Exchange* (May 9, 2014), http://jjie.org/at-wits-end- scared-straight-programs-remain- popular-among-parents-despite- warnings/106811.

7. This section is based on my essay "Obama's Pre-Cooked Goose," *Washington Monthly* (January 22, 2015), http://washington monthly.com/2015/01/22/ obamas-pre-cooked-goose.

8. Congressional Budget Office, *Revisions to CBO's Projection of Potential Output since 2007* (Washington, DC: Congressional Budget Office, February 2014), 3, http://www.cbo.gov/publication/ 45150.

9. For an analysis of performance management systems, see Robert D. Behn, *The PerformanceStat Potential: A Leadership Strategy for Producing Results* (Washington, DC: Brookings Institution, 2014).

10. See Centers for Disease Control and Prevention, PulseNet, https://www.cdc.gov/pulsenet.

11. Jim Lynch, "DEQ Fires Worker Who Supervised Flint's Water," *The Detroit News* (February 5, 2016), http://www.detroitnews .com/story/news/michigan/flint-water-crisis/2016/02/05/flint-water-crisis/79888340; Jim Lynch and Jacob Carah, "Attorney: Ex-State Water Regulator 'Did Nothing Wrong,'" *The Detroit News* (August 3, 2016), http:// www.detroitnews.com/story/ news/michigan/flint-water-crisis/2016/08/03/flint-water-court/88005426.

12. "Lead Testing Results for Water Sampled by Residents," http:// flintwaterstudy.org/information-for-flint-residents/results-for-citizen-testing-for-lead-300-kits (from the intensive analysis performed by Virginia Tech scientists led by Dr. Jeffrey Parks).

13. Lynch, "DEQ Fires Worker Who Supervised Flint's Water."

14. Stephan Braig, Biniam Gebre, and Andrew Sellgren, *Strengthening Risk Management in the U.S. Public Sector* (Washington, DC: McKinsey & Company, May 2011), 1, https:// www.mckinsey.com/~/media/ mckinsey/dotcom/client_service/ Risk/Working%20papers/28_ WP_Risk_management_in_the_ US_public_sector.ashx.

15. U.S. Government Accountability Office, *Enterprise Risk Management: Selected Agencies' Experience Illustrates Good Practices in Managing Risk* (December 2016), http://gao .gov/assets/690/681342.pdf.

16. For the story of how this happened, see Donald F. Kettl, *System under Stress: The Challenge to 21st Century Governance,* 3rd ed. (Thousand Oaks, CA: CQ Press, 2013); and John Tozzi, "How Healthcare.gov Botched $600 Million Worth of Contracts," *Bloomberg* (September 15, 2015), http://www.bloomberg .com/news/articles/2015-09-15/ how-healthcare-gov-botched-600-million-worth-of-contracts.

17. See Louise K. Comfort, Arjen Boin, and Chris C. Demchak, eds., *Designing Resilience: Preparing for Extreme Events* (Pittsburgh: University of Pittsburgh Press, 2010).

18. Gene Kranz, *Failure Is Not an Option: Mission Control from Mercury to Apollo 13 and Beyond* (New York: Simon & Schuster, 2009).

19. Judith Rodin, *The Resilience Dividend: Being Strong in a World Where Things Go Wrong* (New York: Public Affairs, 2014), 3.

20. Global Resilience Partnership, http://www.globalresilience partnership.org.

21. Federal Emergency Management Agency, "Hurricane Pam Exercise Concludes" (July 23, 2004),

http://www.fema.gov/news-release/2004/07/23/hurricane-pam-exercise-concludes.

22. Deseve, *Enhancing the Government's Decision-Making*, 22.

23. Donald F. Kettl, *The Next Government of the United States: Why Our Institutions Fail Us and How to Fix Them* (New York: Norton, 2009).

3

Tell the Story

T he Big Five questions we explored in the last chapter frame the issues to which policymakers need answers. But digging into the data isn't enough, because data never speak for themselves. That's a first lesson that all good policy analysts learn, sometimes only when they learn the lesson the hard way after a few efforts that go nowhere. And it's even more true for busy policymakers, for whom data can be a foreign language—and who, after all, aren't really sure they *need* the data to begin with.

Suppose you're tracking crimes in Los Angeles. You're interested in what's happening in Hollywood. Policymakers can scan the list of crimes on the police blotter (see Figure 3.1). It's hard enough to make sense of crime in Hollywood on that one day. When the list grows to pages and pages, it's impossible to know what's happening. Is crime going up or down? Is it concentrated in some neighborhoods? Are there lots of small crimes? Are there mainly property crimes or violent crimes against individuals? That's impossible to tell from scanning the data—but that, of course, is what policymakers (and citizens) want to know. The *Los Angeles Times* ran a project to translate crime statistics into trends and maps (see Figure 3.2), and that made the data come alive. There were a bit more than three crimes against property for every crime against a person. There hadn't been major changes in the pattern of crimes over the previous three months. And the map made it possible to find out just *where* the crimes were taking place—with famous Sunset Boulevard a hot zone. Anyone trying to make sense of crime in the neighborhood would know *much* more by looking at the map than by scanning page after page of mind-numbing numbers. Anyone interested in tracking what's going on could choose different dates, different time periods, different neighborhoods—and zoom down to individual blocks to get a good fix on the L.A. crime story.

FIGURE 3.1 • Crimes in Hollywood, July 26, 2016

Carmen and Franklin	Grand theft auto	July 26, 11:45 p.m.
Sycamore Avenue and Hollywood Boulevard *(Deleted)*	Aggravated assault	July 26, 10:35 p.m.
5700 block of Harold Way *(Deleted)*	Aggravated assault	July 26, 10:30 p.m.
5700 block of Harold Way *(Deleted)*	Aggravated assault	July 26, 10:30 p.m.
6100 block of West Sunset Boulevard	Theft	July 26, 8:30 p.m.
1400 block of North Alta Vista Boulevard	Burglary	July 26, 7:45 p.m.
1500 block of North Cahuenga Boulevard	Theft	July 26, 6 p.m.
1500 block of North Gordon Street	Theft	July 26, 2:30 p.m.
7700 block of Hollywood Boulevard	Burglary	July 26, 9:30 a.m.
7700 block of Hollywood Boulevard	Burglary	July 26, 7 a.m.
Hollywood Boulevard and Schrader	Robbery	July 26, 12:40 a.m.
800 block of Wilcox Avenue	Theft	July 26, 12:01 a.m.

Source: "Mapping L.A.," *Los Angeles Times* (July 26, 2016), http://maps.latimes.com/neighborhoods/neighborhood/hollywood/crime.

Filters

Data can't speak on their own. But in the right language, they can tell a powerful story. The key is good *data visualization:* translating data to pictures of all kinds, from graphs and charts to maps and other forms of infographics. That's the magic of translating long pages in the crime blotter to maps that bring the information alive. It's the key to knowing.

From the point of view of policymakers, policy problems are continuous and seamless. They focus on problems that occur where people live. The process of knowing, however, is often segmented and compartmentalized. That's because different analysts—and different kinds of analysis—bring different filters. This can elevate some questions and push others off the table. Knowing requires making the right connections so policymakers get the story—the whole story—and don't have to worry about tripping over boundary battles or finding that important issues get left out.

Different puzzles. Table 3.1 shows that the Big Five connect to different puzzles, as we saw in the last chapter. They link to different stages of the policy process, before policymakers make decisions (with forecasts), as they implement policies

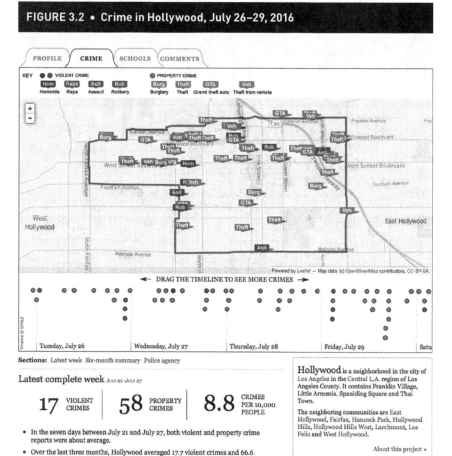

FIGURE 3.2 • Crime in Hollywood, July 26–29, 2016

Source: "Mapping L.A.," *Los Angeles Times* (July 26, 2016), http://maps.latimes.com/neighborhoods/neighborhood/hollywood/crime.

(with performance management), as they assess results (with program evaluation), and as they seek to avoid risks and maximize resilience (at every stage—before bad things happen). But different players tend to be involved at these different stages, with analysts in staff offices focusing on issues before and after program implementation, and front-line managers working on implementation issues themselves. It can often prove very hard to connect information assessing the pre- and post-implementation issues with the implementation process itself. There are different people, working in very different offices and focusing on very different problems, and they often simply don't talk to each other.

Different disciplines. Then there's the challenge of having experts from different disciplines talking with each other. Even economists often have trouble connecting.

TABLE 3.1 • Filters in the Big Five Questions

	Puzzle	Stage of the policy process	Dominant discipline
Hindsight	Program evaluation	Post-implementation	Microeconomics; history
Foresight	Forecasts	Pre-implementation	Macroeconomics
Results	Performance management	Midst of implementation	Public management; history
Risk	Exposure to loss, danger, harm	All stages—solve problems before they happen	Specialized hybrid: finance, management, engineering, information technology, cybersecurity, communications, talent management; history
Resilience	Bouncing back after failure	All stages—solve problems before they happen	Specialized hybrid: leadership, engineering, information technology, architecture, sociology, management, talent management; history

Source: Author created.

They tend to focus on foresight and hindsight. But foresight, especially forecasts based on economic trends, tends to be the province of macroeconomists (who specialize in the whole economy). Microeconomists (who work on individual market segments) tend to focus on hindsight, especially program evaluations and benefit-cost analyses. Economists working in the two branches of economics tend to fly in separate orbits, focusing on different puzzles with different techniques (sometimes coated with undisguised disdain). Then there's an even more fundamental problem: economists talking to non-economists. Many people just don't like economics, period. Stephen Moore, a conservative economist who advised President Donald Trump, quoted Berkeley economist Christina Romer, who headed President Obama's Council of Economic Advisers, as telling an old joke: "There are two kinds of students: those who hate economics and those who really hate economics." And Moore added, "It's true."[1] Economists can have a hard enough time taking to each other. Non-economists can have a hard time hearing what they have to say—or even wanting to listen.

That can especially be the case for connecting the evidence on decisions (hindsight and foresight) and implementation (results). Economists tend to focus on getting the most bang for the buck in decision making. It's not that they believe implementation isn't important. It's just that they see decisions as *more* important because they set the framework for everything else. For decades of policy debates, however, those studying implementation have repeatedly pointed to the fact that decisions aren't self-executing. Implementation is hard work. In fact, in one of the classic works on implementation, Jeffrey L. Pressman and Aaron Wildavsky examined the fate of an economic development program designed in Washington that foundered in California. The book's subtitle—a story in itself—lays bare the problem: "How Great Expectations in Washington Are Dashed in Oakland; or, Why It's Amazing That Federal Programs Work at All, This Being a Saga of the Economic Development Administration as Told by Two Sympathetic Observers Who Seek to Build Morals on a Foundation of Ruined Hopes."[2] Not only did big decisions not produce the results that decision makers intended. The big problem, Pressman and Wildavsky found, was that decision makers didn't pay much attention to implementation. Analysis focused on decisions rarely connects with the analysis required to get results.

Then there's the challenge of assessing risk and resilience. The Big Five questions are on a different plain than the puzzles about decisions and implementation. They ask what could go wrong and how the system might bounce back. Analysis of risk and resilience draws on many disciplines, including many far beyond the traditional policy-related disciplines of economics, political science, and public administration and management. The wide range of disciplines shown in Table 3.1 have added a vast amount of useful texture and evidence. But if economists sometimes have trouble talking to each other, it's often much, much harder to connect the insights of so many different disciplines to a single policy chain. For academics, these are always interesting intellectual puzzles. But for a citizen looking for a seamless experience with government, for programs that work, and for resilience when they don't, the different approaches of different barriers can sometimes create barriers. The patience of decision makers can often wear thin waiting for experts to work out their disciplinary differences.

Different puzzles, different disciplines, one set of programs, one collection of citizens (and taxpayers). The challenge is building the evidence so we know what to do and telling the story so policymakers know how to do it. Those are the fundamental challenges of data visualization: translating what we know for those who need to act.

Seeing Data

Data about the Big Five questions rarely speak clearly on their own. The data often fall on the desks of both analysts and policymakers like the crime chart in Figure 3.1. There's often a cascade of information, which on the surface seems like it would probably be useful but whose meaning is just not clear. How can analysts turn this stuff into the stuff of knowing? How can they tell the story that's in the data, sometimes hidden? There's a host of ways in which they can extract meaning from data.

Statistics

Since time immemorial, analysts have been compiling data to make sense of big issues dealing with government. What's new now? Big problems often come with even bigger data, and decision makers need to find ways of taking small bites of these issues. They seek shorthand ways of describing big piles of complex numbers, which we call *descriptive statistics*, and drawing conclusions about uncertainties in these piles of numbers, which we call *inferential statistics*. The first cut at making sense of data comes with the descriptive statistics. How many crimes occurred in Hollywood last week—and is this an unusual week (that is, is the count of crimes higher or lower than the average)? If the crime count is higher or lower, how atypical is it (that is, how does the weekly crime count vary, and is last week's count relatively unusual)? In the last week of July 2016, for example, there were 17 violent crimes against people (assaults and robberies, for example) and 58 property crimes (such as thefts, burglaries, and grand theft auto, which gave the name to the super-popular video game). That compares with 17.7 violent crimes and 66.6 property crimes, on average, over the previous three months. No crime is good, but the last week of July wasn't an especially unusual week.

Basic statistics are very important. Faced with big piles of numbers, the first question everyone, from analyst to policymaker to citizen, asks is: What's the average? Is my baby's weight average? Is my child reading above or below the grade average? What's my college grade point average, and how does it compare with my classmates'? Is my dog smarter than average? A Google search for "average" produces 1.2 billion hits. It's hard to find a more popular or basic way of making sense of numbers. And everyone, of course, wants to think of themselves as above average—at least on the good things. Consider these news stories:

- "The Federal Workforce, Where Everyone's Performance Gets Rave Reviews." The *Washington Post* reported that "in the ranks of the federal government, 99 percent are really good at their jobs—and almost two-thirds exceed expectations or do outstanding work."[3]
- "California Pensions Take Above-Average Tax Bite." A watchdog website noted, "California pension funds take a bigger share of tax revenue than the national state average, a research website shows. Why the growing costs are outpacing the norm is not completely clear."[4]
- "Waterline Breaks Well below Average This Year across Tulsa." *Tulsa World* told readers that breaks in city water pipes were much lower. In January, for example, the average number of water line breaks is 167. In January 2016, there were just 67. City officials attributed the decline to friendly weather, with constant rainfall that prevented the lines from going through wet/dry cycles. And they pointed out that this would save taxpayers a substantial amount of money.[5]

- "Wyoming: 'More Guns per Capita than Any State,' below Average Gun-Related Murders." The conservative website Brietbart reported, "Wyoming has 'more guns per capita than any state'—yet they have a gun-related murder rate that is below the national average." One local sheriff applauded the fact because he saw "the armed citizenry as a means of augmenting the 'handful of deputies' he has at his disposal."[6]
- And then there's the Lake Wobegon effect, named after a fictional town popularized by Garrison Keillor on his long-running public radio show. "Welcome to Lake Wobegon," he'd say, "where all the women are strong, all the men are good-looking, and all the children are above average."

Averages are tremendously useful. But they convey limited information. It's great to know whether things and people—and policymakers—are higher or lower than average. But these basic statistics don't tell us the most important things. First, the "why" question: What has caused the numbers? And then the "what" question: If policymakers wanted to act to change things, what could they do—and how sure could they be that doing something would have the effects they want? Moving past descriptive statistics, like averages, to inferential statistics, like t-tests and regression analysis, can provide good answers to these questions.

But the results of these tests are often hard to translate to people who don't work in them all the time. A Google News search for "regression" shows more news stories on baseball (Are some teams likely to regress in their performance?) and babies (Are my baby's sleep habits likely to regress—and am I likely to get more tired?) than on public policy issues.

Consider the question Australians worried about in 2016: whether their dollar was likely to move higher against the American dollar, which could make it more expensive to buy imported goods. Detailed inferential statistics, provided on background by Goldman Sachs analyst Robin Brooks, suggested yes—with warnings. As Brooks explained, "We periodically use regression models to map things like interest differentials, commodity prices and risk appetite into exchange rates. These models are always subject to a large grain of salt, but they can be helpful in digesting the myriad drivers of FX [foreign exchange]." But analysts working for BNP Paribas, a major French bank, concluded that its research showed that the Australian dollar was likely to get weaker.[7] The implication for policymakers? The Australian dollar might go up. It might go down. Experts disagreed. And their work was buried in sophisticated statistical models hard for most policymakers to translate—and, in this case, hidden behind website paywalls.

The research is invaluable. It can provide important clues about the future. Careful analysts need to know how to use these tools, and use them well. But it's hard to get these tools to tell the story on their own, or to tell a clear story. Either they leave out things that policymakers want to know, or they provide information that's hard for policymakers to digest. The data don't speak for themselves, and to know what to do, policymakers need help.

Charts

Some help often comes through graphs and charts that everyone knows—or should know—how to create using spreadsheet programs like Microsoft's Excel and Apple's Numbers. With a few clicks, analysts can transform a pile of dense data into attractive pie charts, line charts, and other tools. The results can be striking. For example, consider Figures 3.3 and 3.4, which show federal spending on entitlements for individuals. Has spending grown? By how much? The charts here show several ways of answering those questions.

It will surprise no one who follows federal budgetary policy and politics that spending for entitlements grew rapidly after World War II—and especially starting in the 1970s, when Medicare and Medicaid became increasingly important and benefits for Social Security grew. But the amount spent each year—what economists call "current dollars"—isn't a good way to compare spending over time. Inflation cuts into the purchasing power of money over time. We can account for that by looking at spending in constant dollars (that is, calculating spending according to the purchasing power in a standard year—in this case, 2009). When displayed in constant dollars, entitlement spending has grown rapidly—but not quite as fast as current dollars.

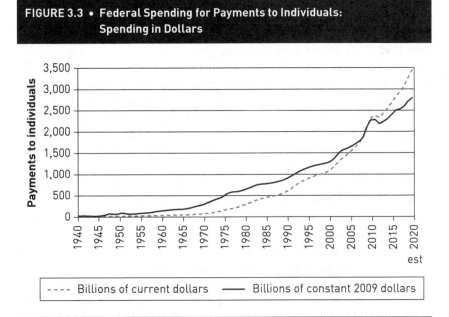

FIGURE 3.3 • **Federal Spending for Payments to Individuals: Spending in Dollars**

Source: U.S. Office of Management and Budget, *Budget of the United States Government, Fiscal Year 2017: Historical Tables*, Table 6.1, https://www.whitehouse.gov/omb/budget/Historicals.

Charting the spending in inflation-adjusted dollars, however, doesn't account for other puzzles. Federal spending overall has grown; has entitlement spending grown as a share of all federal spending? And the economy has grown over the same period; how much of the economy does entitlement spending take up? Here the story gets even more interesting (see Figure 3.4). In 1960, entitlements accounted for just over a quarter (26.3 percent) of all federal spending. By 2020, economists projected, the number would rise to 70.3 percent. That's almost three times as large a size of the overall pie. What about entitlements as a share of the economy? In the same period, they grew by almost four times, from 4.5 percent to 15.7 percent.

Now, let's think about how best to compare these findings. Table 3.2 shows percentage changes for each of these measures, over the sixty-year period from 1960 to 2020. What's the best measure? The numbers range from almost 15,000 percent down to 168 percent. There's no doubt that entitlement spending has grown. But by how much? What do we know about this?

The answer depends on how we frame the question. And skillful analysts know that they can frame the question depending on the answer they want. Different measures produce different conclusions, some far more frightening than others.

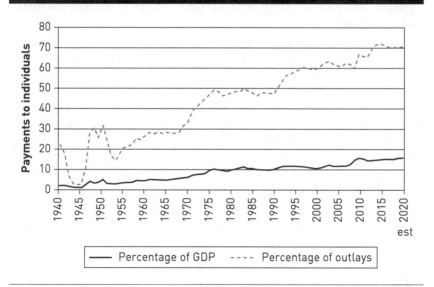

FIGURE 3.4 • Federal Spending for Payments to Individuals: Spending as a Share of All Federal Outlays and of the Economy

Percentage of GDP   ---- Percentage of outlays

Source: U.S. Office of Management and Budget, *Budget of the United States Government, Fiscal Year 2017: Historical Tables*, Table 6.1, https://www.whitehouse.gov/omb/budget/Historicals.

TABLE 3.2 • Percentage Changes in Payments for Individuals	
	Change: 1960–2020
Billions of current dollars	14,813.5%
Billions of constant 2009 dollars	1,971.3%
Percentage of GDP	251.1%
Percentage of outlays	168.4%

Source: Author created.

Different charts produce different conclusions from each other—and different from the table. Furthermore, that's before we tinker with the axes, which we can use to alter the shape of the curves and make changes look larger or smaller. Tell me what kind of conclusion you want, and I can draw you a graph that supports it. There are countless examples of analysts who have done just that. And when an analyst works for an organization with a clear point of view, the signals about what the "right" answer is to a problem—how best to present data in a way that reinforces the organization's mission and ideology—can be inescapable. That, in turn, often raises very tough ethical issues for analysts: Is my obligation to my employer, who pays my salary? Or to the truth? And if the latter, is the "truth" ever really clear?

This is one reason why Mark Twain coined the now-famous line, "There are lies, damn lies, and statistics." To which he added, "Facts are stubborn, but statistics are more pliable."[8] That's a bit too cynical, of course. Analysts have a large collection of very sophisticated statistical tools to assess underlying facts and significance tests to determine how solid their conclusions are. But there's often great cynicism about statistics, charts, and the underlying realities they seek to capture. And this is also part of the reason why it's often so hard for policymakers to get comfortable with the numbers they get. They often fear that the numbers and charts they see have been cooked to make a particular point. Except when statistics remain clouded in uncertainty. Harry S. Truman famously said, "Give me a one-handed economist! All my economists say, ''On the one hand? On the other.'''[9]

Statistics are invaluable to help us know things. But policymakers often don't know what they can know from them.

Maps

Most statistics and charts have a common limitation: they live in a two-dimensional world. To be sure, there are 3-D options for some charts, but they are intended to dress up presentations, not add meaning. Edward R. Tufte, the modern master of data visualization, explained that "the world portrayed on our information displays is caught up in the two-dimensionality of the endless flatlands of paper and video screens." All the interesting worlds live in 3-D, fueled by the fourth dimension of time.[10] The trick is capturing multiple dimensions on flat pages, and creating images that communicate them clearly and persuasively to policymakers who have to decide what to do with them.

The point here is that there are some things we'd like to know that aren't captured in statistics. Statistics are very good at capturing key dimensions of data, like the average. They are essential for exploring causality—which changes lead to which outcomes. But they often fall short on other things that matter. Just *where* do things happen? Citizens, and the policymakers who serve them, want to know what's happening where they live. Maps are great for doing just that. As we saw in Figure 3.2, dealing with crime in Hollywood, maps can tell what kinds of things are happening where. They can also quickly lead to important questions. Are different kinds of problems, like crimes of violence and crimes against property, related? And when maps are compared over time, it's possible to see if some kinds of problems are growing in some areas. Are the number and severity of crimes escalating? Are some streets becoming more crime-prone? Maps help provide answers, and they have several important advantages:

- *Maps tell the story policymakers and citizens care about most.* Policymakers tend to represent individual communities. They'll surely be interested in the overall patterns of the data, but what they'll care about most is how a program affects their neighborhood, district, town, or state. Maps tell the story that policymakers want most to hear. And they also talk to citizens, who, after all, live in neighborhoods and not in programs, which are so often the focus of analysts' work.

- *Maps can provide quick snapshots of issues.* It usually takes time to generate a sufficient amount of data to use statistics, especially to make use of the more sophisticated techniques. Maps can provide quick snapshots, even of week-by-week trends in crime or hour-by-hour feedback on which streets have been plowed following a snowstorm. After a big blizzard, few things are more important to citizens (and the public officials who represent them) than knowing how long they'll have to wait to get out of their driveways.

- *Maps fit some issues better than others.* Statistics are far better in exploring causality, in making predictions about future trends, and in assessing the effectiveness of policy initiatives. But maps are often much better in charting patterns of policy implementation, where traditional statistics often fall short.

- *Maps can suggest patterns and connections.* Even a relatively untrained eye can scan a map, see a concentration of dots, and ask, "I wonder what's going on there?" From hot spots of crime to trends in garbage collection, maps can help visualize patterns.

- *Maps can suggest connections.* Maps can help even novices ask questions about connections between programs. In the Obama administration's stimulus program, designed to jump-start the economy following the 2008 economic collapse, the White House produced an online mapping system that allowed anyone anywhere to see where the money was going. The administration wanted to ensure that the money was being spent well—and that it could protect itself from charges of waste and abuse. So, to promote transparency, it launched an online mapping system to chart every project, and citizens could look up projects in any part of the country. At a presentation on the system, a college freshman looked at a map of her home town for a few seconds, saw a collection of dots representing different projects, and asked precisely the right question: "I wonder if they're talking to each other?" Maps make such insights possible in a way unlike anything else.
- *Maps tell stories that stick.* Pages of data or tests of statistical significance don't have nearly the impact of a map that shows citizens—and their elected officials—what's happening in their neighborhood. Maps help tell the story because they portray complex issues as pictures, in ways that allow citizens to zero in on the places they care about most.

In some cases, maps and related charts can bring the story to life, including showing the rise and fall of important forces over time. The *New York Times,* for example, created a chart showing how financial giants shrank, and then grew, during the financial crisis. The paper's graphic designed the animation to show how the entire financial sector changed, from the pre-crisis days in 2007 to the tough days of recovery in 2009, and how some companies weathered the storm better than others.[11] It's also possible to create charts that show changes in important variables over time using colors, bubbles, and basic Excel charts (like line, bar, and stacked bar charts). We won't look in detail in this book at tools for creating charts and maps—there are other books that do so in far greater detail, and there are great software programs to make the job easier.[12] For our purposes here, it's important to have a clear sense of the contributions that maps and charts can bring to policy debates.

We'll explore some of the challenges of visualization in the next chapter. For now, though, there's an important lesson: the technology can get out of hand, and what's technically possible doesn't always speak clearly. Simpler is almost always better.

Metadata

Important findings can sometimes come through large piles of data, including *metadata,* which can supply important insights from other data. This information can sometimes come from unexpected places. Google, for example, tracks the searches on its website and packages that information in ways that provide fascinating insights. Google Trends (https://www.google.com/trends), for example, shows the stories trending at the moment, either worldwide or in individual countries. Government's use of metadata has sometimes proven very contentious. Indeed, the National Security Agency's review of telephone records during the 2000s, disclosed by former employee Edward Snowden, provoked enormous controversy.

But careful and ethical use of metadata can provide valuable data. For example, citizens and journalists make thousands of Freedom of Information Act requests. A thorough look at what they are asking for, what's available, and what's not can streamline government's quest for greater transparency by helping managers focus on the information they most need to package and disclose. Government agencies can scan emails for clues about who might be trying to break into sensitive data systems through phishing and spoofing. As the government's data stockpile explodes, metadata analysis can help identify which data are used most often (and therefore ought to have the first priority for being backed up and supported) and which data might be duplicative (and therefore could be purged—some studies suggest that duplicate data might be as much as 20 to 40 percent of all the data government agencies have on hand). The strategy could help the government determine which data to migrate to new systems and which to purge. Moreover, by looking both at what users are trying to find and what data agencies have on hand, metadata analysis can help create better indexes to help users, inside and outside government, find useful data.[13] There's no better way of telling the story than making far better use of the data we have and saving far more money in how we use it. We often don't know what we know—or even what sources we have on which we can grow knowledge.

Metadata and data visualization, moreover, can be married to produce powerful findings. And, as is often the case, Google is trying to get there first. Google Trends, for example, allows researchers to discover the Halloween costumes for which people in different parts of the country search. In 2015, for example, Google's "Frightgeist" page found that the most frequent costume search in Portland, Maine, was a pirate. In Grand Junction, Colorado, it was a hippie. In Yuma, Arizona: Wonder Woman. Figure 3.5 shows that Batman was most searched in Juneau, Alaska. (In 2016, however, Harley Quinn leapt into the lead in Portland, and a princess was the most popular costume in Grand Junction.)

The Google Trends tool also provides invaluable policy insight, from how the world responded to the November 13, 2015, terrorist attack in Paris to how mass shootings in 2015 affected search terms like "gun control" and "gun shop"—and how that varied in different states, compared with overall searches for the entire year. Such metadata can provide keen insight into how citizens react to events, what policy concerns are most on their minds, and what policymakers can know about which actions are most likely to be best received by citizens.

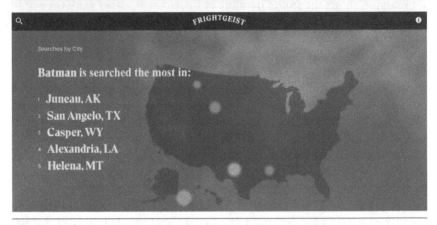

FIGURE 3.5 • Google's Frightgeist Page for Batman Costumes, 2016

Source: "Frightgeist," https://frightgeist.withgoogle.com. Google Trends.

Open Data

New ways of telling the story have emerged through the "open data" movement, in which data producers make the basic data available to other analysts, reporters, citizens, and policymakers. Open data creates opportunity for enormous creativity in extracting meaning from the data, often in ways that the data originators could never have imagined. And open data often vastly increases the supply of data as well—so open data often makes for bigger data. Open data expert Dennis D. McDonald explains that this movement has evolved through three stages:

- *Open Data 1.0:* Governments put data online, through a central web catalog. Governments can accompany the increased transparency with additional tools, like the ability to download data and visualize it through charts and maps.
- *Open Data 2.0:* Governments move to a next phase, characterized by regular data updates, information about the context and meaning of the data, increased standardization of data so users can more easily make comparisons, and stronger tech support.
- *Open Data 3.0:* Government officials embrace data as a strategy for engaging citizens, with the expectation that all data are open unless there are compelling reasons to make them closed (such as for reasons of national security, privacy, and corporate competition).[14]

Open data builds on several premises. First, it can make government programs more accountable by making their operations more transparent. If anyone who cares about a program can see what it's doing and where it's doing it, accountability is stronger. Second, it can make programs more effective by increasing and broadening knowledge about what programs are accomplishing. No one gets everything right the first time. Increasing feedback—and increasing the number of stakeholders who have access to information to provide feedback—can improve a program's quality. Third, it can open up new and unexpected ways of using data to improve programs and services. For example, Loudoun County, Virginia (the county where Washington's Dulles International Airport is located), automated its vast collection of maps and made them available to the public starting in the late 1980s. Since then, it saved $700,000 in selecting a site for a new landfill, especially by charting how close proposed sites were to population centers and water resources. The county has used the system to manage requests for building permits and to improve the response of emergency vehicles. And to help the county's mushrooming beer industry, the county produced an online app to help farmers determine the best locations for growing hops (which turns out to be in farmland in the western part of the county, near the West Virginia border).[15]

The pursuit of open data has grown into a movement, with principles laid out by advocates at a meeting in Sebastopol, California, in 2007 (see Table 3.3). And it's produced an amazing array of applications, from finding public libraries and tracking whether your flight is on time to finding the best elder-care services and finding banks that invest their money in their local communities.[16] To locate alternative fueling stations, drivers can go to a U.S. Department of Energy website and find locations anywhere in the country (see Figure 3.6). The state of Pennsylvania put a dozen of its datasets online, accessible through a single portal.[17] Data increasingly has become the language of policy—and open data has become the driver of innovation.

But openness isn't easy, and building the corral to hold it can close the road to open data. In the spring of 2016, a California state legislative committee approved a bill that would have allowed state and local governments to copyright their data

---

TABLE 3.3 • Principles of Open Government Data

- *Complete.* All public data are available, and all available data are public.
- *Primary.* All data, to the degree possible, come from the source, without any intermediary filtering.
- *Timely.* All data are made available as quickly as possible.
- *Accessible.* All data are available to the broadest range of users, including through the Internet.
- *Machine processable.* All data are structured so computer programs can easily manage them.
- *Nondiscriminatory.* All data are available to anyone.
- *Nonproprietary.* All data are available through formats that no one can exclusively control.

Source: "The Annotated 8 Principles of Open Government Data," https://opengovdata.org.

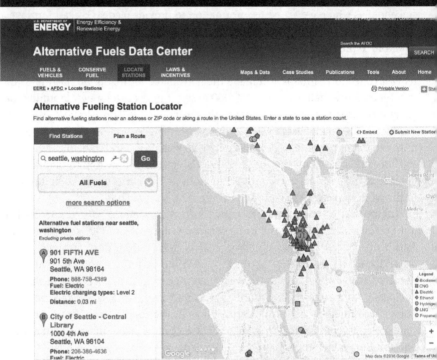

FIGURE 3.6 • Alternative Fueling Stations in Seattle

Source: U.S. Department of Energy, "Alternative Fuels Data Center," http://www.afdc.energy.gov/loca stations/results?utf8=✓&location=seattle%2C+washington&fuel=all&private=false&planned=fals owner=all&payment=all&radius=false&radius_miles=5.

and reports. Private contractors working for these governments would have had their intellectual property—from reports and maps to studies and data—protected from public use without paying license fees. The debate is important. On the one hand, private contractors argue that they build their businesses on the capacity to do important work, and that if they give it away for free it would undermine their livelihoods. On the other hand, taxpayer dollars pay for this work and, the argument goes, taxpayers ought to have free access to the data they've already bought. In this case, the California state senate removed the provision and kept the data open. But the underlying question—just how open should open data be?—remains the subject of fierce debate.[18]

Making Data Speak

Data are essential to telling the story of what matters in public policy. But since the late 1980s, ways to do that have exploded, thanks to the rise of the Internet, computers, and mobile devices. There are more data and new kinds of data. There's a growing expectation that more data should be public and that public data should be used more to enhance the performance and accountability of government programs. There's a rapidly accelerating number of ways the data can be put to work to help us see things—from where best to produce beer to how long we'll have to wait in the airport security line—that previously were invisible, or very hard to know.

The traditional forms of data analysis, including descriptive statistics and tools to measure causality, remain very important. But these new sources of data, along with the tools to analyze and visualize them, have vastly increased our ability to tell the story and make data speak. They've democratized knowledge in ways that were unimaginable at the dawn of the computer age. And they've posed new challenges, both for accessing information and ensuring that the data enhance democracy and accountability. The tools for managing these data, from relatively straightforward apps like Excel, to intermediate systems like Google Trends, to more complex mapping programs like ArcGIS, sketch out a new frontier of making data talk. Digging deeply into each of these tools is the subject of whole books in themselves.

But from this remarkable swirl of new strategies and techniques, there is a set of basic questions. Can we believe what the data tell us? How can we communicate what the data seem to say in ways that others—especially those (like policymakers) who are super busy and perhaps not as technically savvy—can grasp what the data mean and what they ought to do about it? And how can the data enhance our democracy, both by making government more effective and by making it easier for citizens to connect with their elected officials on the things that matter most to them? Those are the key puzzles of telling the story. And they set up the next question in our search for knowing: Once we try to tell the story, how can we *sell* it? That's the question we turn to in Chapter 4.

Notes

1. Stephen Moore, "Why Americans Hate Economics," *Wall Street Journal* (August 19, 2011), http://www.wsj.com/articles/SB100014240531119035969045765145528773886 10.

2. Jeffrey L. Pressman and Aaron B. Wildavsky, *Implementation: How Great Expectations in Washington Are Dashed in Oakland; or, Why It's Amazing That Federal Programs Work at All, This Being a Saga of the Economic Development Administration as Told by Two Sympathetic Observers Who Seek to Build Morals on a Foundation of Ruined Hopes* (Berkeley: University of California Press, 1973).

3. Lisa Rein, "The Federal Workforce, Where Everyone's Performance Gets Rave Reviews,"

Washington Post (June 13, 2016), https://www.washingtonpost.com/news/powerpost/wp/2016/06/13/heres-the-news-from-the-federal-government-where-everyone-is-above-average-way-above.

4. Calpensions, "California Pensions Take Above-Average Tax Bite" (July 5, 2016), https://calpensions.com/2016/07/05/california-pensions-take-above-average-tax-bite.

5. Jarrel Wade, "Waterline Breaks Well below Average This Year across Tulsa," *Tulsa World* (August 10, 2016), http://www.tulsaworld.com/news/government/waterline-breaks-well-below-average-this-year-across-tulsa/article_816e50c5-fe38-525f-9a1b-38dfe1e45d70.html.

6. Awr Hawkins, "Wyoming: 'More Guns per Capita than Any State,' below Average Gun-Related Murders" (August 4, 2016), http://www.breitbart.com/big-government/2016/08/04/wyoming-more-guns-per-capita-than-any-state-below-average-gun-related-murders.

7. Sam Coventry, "The AUD/USD Rally Is Likely to Extend Say Goldman Sachs, CIBC Markets, Not So Say BNP Paribas," *Daily Institutional Research* (August 10, 2016), https://www.poundsterlinglive.com/forecastsnow-by-pound-sterling-live/5295-australian-dollar-to-head-higher-goldmans-and-cibc.

8. "Statistics," Brainy Quote, http://www.brainyquote.com/search_results.html?q=statistics.

9. "Famous Quotes by Harry S. Truman," Book of Famous Quotes, http://www.famous-quotes.com/author.php?aid=7325.

10. Edward R. Tufte, *Envisioning Information* (Cheshire, CT: Graphics Press, 1990), 12; and *The Visual Display of Quantitative Data* (Cheshire, CT: Graphics Press, 1983).

11. Karl Russell and Shan Carter, "How the Giants of Finance Shrank, Then Grew, under the Financial Crisis," *New York Times* (September 12, 2009), http://www.nytimes.com/interactive/2009/09/12/business/financial-markets-graphic.html?_r=0.

12. For example, see Tufte, *Envisioning Information* and *The Visual Display of Quantitative Data*; Cole Nussbaumer Knaflic, *Storytelling with Data: A Data Visualization Guide for Business Professionals* (Hoboken, NJ: Wiley, 2015); and John W. Foreman, *Data Smart: Using Data Science to Transform Information into Insight* (Indianapolis: Wiley, 2014).

13. Jim McGann, "4 More Ways Government Can Use Metadata Right Now," *Government Technology* (September 5, 2013), http://www.govtech.com/data/

4-More-Ways-the-Government-Can-Use-Metadata-Right-Now.html.

14. Dennis D. McDonald, "Is Your Organization Ready for the Third Age of Open Data?" (March 30, 2015), https://dennis-mcdonald-58qa.squarespace.com/managing-technology/is-your-organization-ready-for-the-third-age-of-open-data.html.

15. Lawrence Stipek, "GIS's Evolving Promise for Local Government," *Governing* (August 12, 2016), http://www.governing.com/blogs/bfc/col-loudoun-county-virginia-gis-improve-decision-making.html; on hop-producing land, see "Suitability Model for Growing Hops in Loudoun County, Virginia," http://loudoungis.maps.arcgis.com/apps/webappviewer/index.html?id=3910bf77cdcf483abea6e01d074045b0.

16. On finding public libraries, see "Public Libraries Survey," Institute of Museum and Library Services, https://www.imls.gov/research-evaluation/data-collection/public-libraries-survey; on flight arrival times, see GateGuru, http://gateguru.com; on elder care, see Happy ElderCare, http://www.happyeldercare.com; on banking local, see BankLocal, http://banklocal.info.

17. See Open Data Pennsylvania, https://data.pa.gov. For an analysis, see Bill Lucia, "Pennsylvania's New Open Data Website Is Now Live," *GovExec.com* (August 22, 2016), http://www.routefifty.com/2016/08/pennsylvania-open-data-wolf/130955/?oref=rf-today-nl.

18. Daniel Castro, "California Came Dangerously Close to Ruining What Makes Open Data 'Open,'" *Government Technology* (September 2, 2016), http://www.govtech.com/opinion/California-Came-Dangerously-Close-Ruining-What-Makes-Open-Data-Open-Opinion.html?mc_cid=3dc1f19f84&mc_eid=9f06441d8a.

Sell the Story

I t's one thing to have a story to tell. It's often quite another to tell it well—to sell the story to those who need to hear it.

Sometimes this step goes very badly. Every student knows the power of PowerPoint, but in the case of the tragic disintegration of the space shuttle *Columbia* in 2003, a *New York Times* writer concluded, "PowerPoint Makes You Dumb."[1] A weak PowerPoint presentation, investigators found, had helped blind NASA officials to the risk the crew faced.

On launch, a piece of insulation foam struck the shuttle and made a small hole in the orbiter's wing. When *Columbia* reentered the atmosphere sixteen days later, very hot gases ate away at that hole until the wing disintegrated, sending the shuttle to Earth and killing all seven crew members. NASA's engineers knew that such collisions between insulation and the shuttle had occurred on three previous launches. In each case, the shuttles returned safely. High-speed cameras captured the impact of the foam on *Columbia's* launch. Engineers knew that the shuttle had been damaged, but they disagreed on how serious a problem the crew faced. How did they communicate the danger? The answer, it turns out, was by PowerPoint. The most important slide, shown to decision makers while *Columbia* was still in orbit, is shown in Figure 4.1. As Edward R. Tufte pointed out in his analysis for the NASA commission investigating the disaster, the slide contained lots of information, but few managers looking at the slide would know that the information in it suggested that the shuttle might be heading toward a disaster. The shuttle crew faced a huge risk, but that fact was buried in the slide's jargon and details. In fact, the investigation board concluded:

> As information gets passed up an organization hierarchy, from people who do analysis to mid-level managers to high-level leadership, key explanations

and supporting information is filtered out. In this context, it is easy to understand how a senior manager might read this PowerPoint slide and not realize that it addresses a life-threatening situation.[2]

Given the nature of the damage and the limited equipment the crew had on board, it wasn't likely that they could have done anything to avoid the disaster. But the

---

FIGURE 4.1 • Briefing Slide Assessing the Risk to *Columbia*

Review of Test Data Indicates Conservatism for Tile Penetration

- The existing SOFT on tile test data used to create Crater was reviewed along with STS-107 Southwest Research data
  - Crater overpredicted penetration of tile coating significantly
    - Initial penetration to described by normal velocity
      - Varies with volume/mass of projectire (e.g., 200f /sec for 3cu. In)
    - Significant energy is required for the softer SOFI particle to penetrate the relatively hard tile
      - Test results do show that it is possible at sufficient mass and velocity
    - Conversely, once tile is penetrated SOFT can cause significant damage
      - Minor variations in total energy (above penetration level) can cause significant tile damage
  - Flight condition is significantly outside of test database
    - Volume of ramp is 1920 cu in vs 3 cu in for test

BOEING   2/21/03   6

"Significant" and "significantly" are used repeatedly, but what is the standard? What would the consequences be?

"It" refers to damage to the protecting tiles, which is potentially more dangerous than it appears on the slide.

The most important point of the slide is at the bottom—that the current conditions are "significantly outside of test database." That means the damage is beyond what the engineers have previously explored—and that they don't know what's going to happen. That is the crucial conclusion, but it's buried in a way that policymakers might not even notice.

Source: Analysis by Edward Tufte, in Columbia Accident Investigation Board, *Report: Volume I* (Washington, D.C.: U.S. Government Printing Office, 2003), 191, http://s3.amazonaws.com/akamai.netstorage/anon .nasa-global/CAIB/CAIB_lowres_full.pdf.

underlying facts are striking: NASA had information at its disposal to know the risks that the crew were facing, but the policymakers making key decisions about the mission didn't know what the engineers knew because the engineers failed to tell and sell the story.

This wasn't the only time that PowerPoint has gotten in the way of clear communication. The Pentagon has had an ongoing problem of creating enough classified bandwidth for officers and decision makers to share mission-critical information. The culprit? Fancy animations and graphics on PowerPoint slides that caused the files to explode in size, with moving tanks and flying planes and complicated transitions between pages. The material was classified, and the mega-files clogged up the Defense Department's intranet. "Applications grow until you fill up the memory you've got," explained General Lance Lord, chief of the Air Force Space Command way back in 2003.[3] This had two effects. The clogged bandwidth made it harder for information-dependent systems to complete their missions. In addition, with more studies and analyses communicated through PowerPoint instead of more detailed written reports, important issues became condensed. As a result, as one insider explained, "in many cases, the briefings are incomprehensible."[4]

If you can't tell it and sell it, there's no way policymakers can know it and do it. It's of little use to have great data and impressive graphics if the information isn't presented in a way that decision makers can see it, digest it, understand it, and know what to do about it. As we've seen throughout this book, data don't speak for themselves. Moreover, analysts often forget that decision makers don't need— or know that they need—analysis to make decisions. They're perfectly capable of using their instincts, common sense, word of mouth, and relatively unproven sources of information when they make decisions. Knowing not only requires wrestling the data to the ground; it requires answering the questions that decision makers need to have answered, in a language that makes sense to them.

Anecdotes

If you spend much time around policymakers, one thing quickly becomes clear: good politicians tell great stories. To get electoral traction, most candidates sell a personal story. In the 2016 presidential campaign, it was Marco Rubio's tale of immigration; Donald Trump's mastery of his real estate universe; Bernie Sanders's rise from service as the mayor of Burlington, Vermont; and Hillary Clinton's work championing health care and women's rights. Most campaign stump speeches have standard jokes, from George W. Bush's self-deprecating wisecracks (at the 2001 Yale commencement, he told graduates, "To the C students, I say, 'You too can be president of the United States'") to the sometimes sharp wit of Barack Obama (when visiting the turbulent Mideast in 2013, he quipped that he was glad to be there because it was "good to get away from Congress").[5] Politicians pride themselves on their ability to connect with their audiences. They do what works. Few things work better than stories. The ones that get big laughs work best of all. And they are the ones that politicians keep repeating. Indeed, that's an important lesson of Donald Trump's presidential campaign: the lines in his stump speeches and Tweets were invariably the ones that got the strongest feedback from his audiences.

In the United Kingdom, analysts have found that the use of stories in major-party conference speeches has dramatically increased. In 1990, there were no anecdotes. In 2007, the speeches by three party leaders had twenty anecdotes, especially "to make things more accessible,"[6] analyst Judi Atkins explained. In fact, anecdotes have not only risen in importance and popularity among elected officials. They've sometimes supplanted more detailed evidence, just as PowerPoint pushed away engineering studies in NASA. As ABC News analyst Matthew Dowd explained, "Anecdotes are used as proof of a certain position without supporting overall evidence or data." That can make it "very difficult sometimes to find the truth when folks are presenting a series of 'irrefutable' anecdotes." Dowd went on, "I believe in the immense power of storytelling and the need for the discovery of anecdotes that can connect people with what is going on in the world." However, he worried, too often the anecdotes are unconnected to data that support them, and that makes them nothing more than political spin. But "when supported by objective evidence, there is nothing more powerful than a good anecdote."[7]

That gets to the core of the knowledge paradox of the 21st century: as problems grow ever more complex and the tsunami of information grows about almost everything, there's a growing need—and an inescapable desire—by policymakers to find stories that simplify the complicated world. A July 2016 poll of state and local leaders found that 65 percent thought their organization was "overwhelmed" by data.[8] Indeed, that's an inescapable dilemma of big data. Swamped with more and more information, they struggle with how best to know what to do.

That goes for both the demand and supply side of policymakers' talk. On the demand side, they need and want stories that bring clarity to the piles of reports and their often conflicting recommendations. Mounting stacks of studies can make it much harder for policymakers to determine what to do. Stories make things simpler. Policymakers are used to connecting with voters with anecdotes that amuse or frighten, so anecdotes prove powerful. Moreover, once they get rooted in a policymaker's head, they can prove very hard to dislodge. New piles of analyses can prove just as troublesome as the first piles did, and they can chase policymakers back to the anecdotes they used to simplify the world to begin with. When trying to sort out the case for going to war in Iraq in 2002, it was much easier for British and American policymakers to latch onto a basic narrative: that Saddam Hussein was a dangerous dictator, he had used weapons of mass destruction on his own people in the past, and he had materials available to manufacture more weapons. Even his denials fed into the narrative, since policymakers believed he was just the kind of leader likely to lie about his capacity and motives. It was an enormous tragedy when the countries went to war only to discover that Saddam's denials had been right all along.

On the supply side, as policymakers try to share information with citizens, there's the same challenge. Reporters love anecdotes, especially when they're connected with pictures and video, in covering complex stories. Charts and numbers don't easily fit televised news. Even when citizens see the full story on tables and charts, it's tough for them to absorb them as they fly past on the web or on television—and even harder to remember them. For example, there's an enormous amount of sophisticated research from randomized controlled trials behind recommendations on which women should get mammograms when. But the recommendations vary with age, family history, and a woman's own medical history. The research isn't clear-cut, and different expert groups disagree (see Figure 4.2). What's a policymaker to do? Putting out the research is one thing. But reporters inevitably search for an individual who can bring an important aspect of the story to life, and that's what individuals tend to remember. In trying to sort out the competing recommendations, the *Wall Street Journal* told the stories of individual women.

The more information and evidence there is, the higher the demand by everyone in the system to bring simplicity and clarity to what the data say. "I see all the data," policymakers often say. "There's a lot of disagreement on what the data show and what I ought to decide. What should I do?" It's much easier to sort

FIGURE 4.2 • Mammogram Screening Guidelines

Seeking Consensus on Mammograms

Some doctors are trying to reconcile various groups' recommendations for what age women should start getting mammograms and how often.

	USPSTF*	ACOG**	American Cancer Society
40s	No specific recommendation	Every year	45+ every year
50–74	Every two years	Every year	Every other year starting at 55
75+	No specific recommendation	No upper age limit for screening	Every other year while life expectancy is 10 years or more

*U.S. Preventive Services Task Force

**American College of Obstetricians and Gynecologists

Source: Sumathi Reddy, "Final Recommendations on When to Start Getting a Mammogram," *Wall Street Journal* (January 11, 2016), http://www.wsj.com/articles/final-recommendations-on-when-to-start-getting-a-mammogram-1452549643.

through the ambiguity on the basis of a handful of real-life stories than to try to decipher complex, often conflicting statistical tables. Once the decision is made, the cascade of anecdotes often continues. Was Obama's Affordable Care Act a success? He pointed to families who got insurance for the first time and individuals with preexisting conditions who were now able to afford care. Critics pointed to individuals who complained that they had faced enormous problems in negotiating the application process and high costs.[9] Warring data often get reduced to competing anecdotes. Sometimes the anecdotes become disconnected from supporting data. And what both policymakers and citizens come to believe can end up depending on how good the stories are and how well they're told.

Knowing can become unmoored from data because of the complexity of problems, the volume of data, the uncertainty inherent in analysis, and the challenge of sorting through ambiguity. The larger the complexity, volume, uncertainty, and ambiguity, the more attractive stories and anecdotes become, for everyone.

And that frames the fundamental question: Is it valid to use anecdotes to convey complex data? Most statisticians would roll out a long list of objections. Anecdotes represent one case instead of a large collection. They aren't the product of randomized controlled trials, statistical tests of significance, or validation against a larger sample of cases. In short, why would any self-respecting analyst use stories in a serious policy debate?

A former Massachusetts state legislator helps detail why. In 1991, he says, he tried to make the case against deregulating the state's rate-setting programs for hospitals. Private markets, his opponents argued, could do a far better job of controlling costs. Everywhere he went, from press conferences to hearings, he brought a nine-inch stack of evidence—peer-reviewed studies—supporting his case. His opponents argued with anecdotes from the real world that showed how they had controlled costs without state regulation. "In the end," the legislator concluded, "their perspective mattered more than the reams of scientific evidence I brought to the debate." The next year, he found himself in the middle of a fierce battle over whether to require insurance companies to pay for bone marrow transplants for breast cancer patients. Researchers said that the treatment's value hadn't been proven. Several women testified how it had saved their lives. Their stories won and the bill became law. More than fifteen years later, controlled experiments demonstrated that bone marrow transplants were very costly, very painful, and no more effective in treating breast cancer patients. As the legislator, John E. McDonough, concluded in a 2001 paper:

> Stories can enable lawmakers to understand a legitimate need for policy change but just as readily can lead them to make bad policy decisions. Stories can bring to life drab data analyses, helping us to visualize problems and opportunities for change. But stories also can lead us down wasteful and dangerous paths and blind us to uncomfortable truths we would prefer to ignore, like the fact that there yet is no easy cure for breast cancer.[10]

Anecdotes have power because of these factors:

- *Simplicity.* Anecdotes invariably are easier to digest than statistics.
- *Clarity.* Stories endure because they bring complex problems to life and give them a human touch.
- *Sticking power.* People remember powerful stories, often much longer than they recall arcane statistics.
- *Values.* Anecdotes stick because they capture and reinforce values.
- *Connection.* Stories help forge a connection between policymakers and citizens in a way that numbers rarely can.

This is surprisingly often the case, even in scientific inquiry. Stephen Jay Gould, the famous Harvard natural scientist, concluded, "So much of science proceeds by telling stories."[11] Battles in science often hinge on battles among ideas. The same, of course, is true in policy battles, as Deborah A. Stone reminds us in *Policy Paradox*.[12] When it comes to battles of ideas, stories often more poignantly capture what the real fight is about.

Thus, storytelling is inevitable, even desirable. Can it be valid? Yes, if the anecdote validly and reliably captures the central truth of the underlying reality. Indeed, that's just what an average (mean or median) does: capture the central tendency of the data. To be sound, anecdotes must be:

- *Valid.* The story must truly and accurately capture the underlying phenomenon.
- *Accountable.* The source for the story must be clear and transparent.
- *Context-based.* The setting for the story must be clear, and the conclusions for the story must match the setting.
- *Digestible.* Stories that are too complex won't stick.
- *Real.* Anecdotes have to be believable, not based on obvious exaggerations or stunts.

For policy analysts, storytelling can be taught by mapping a message, building a story, getting good visuals, and making the tale real to an audience. NASA, in fact, has employed a teacher-in-chief, whose job is to help agency employees find creative ways of translating the exceptionally complex work of rocket scientists into stories with which people—especially members of Congress—can connect. (And how cool of a job is that?) For example, a genuine rocket scientist, Miguel Roman, made headlines during the 2014 holiday season by showing how NASA's satellite imagery can see holiday lights from space, especially in the Washington, D.C., area (see Figure 4.3). The result was not only a stunning series of pictures; it was an opportunity to showcase NASA's emerging work in assessing the human impact on the planet, including the ways religious observances change energy usage—NASA found similar changes in light levels in Cairo during the Muslim holiday of Ramadan. "If we're going to reduce these [greenhouse gas] emissions,

FIGURE 4.3 • Holiday Lights from Space

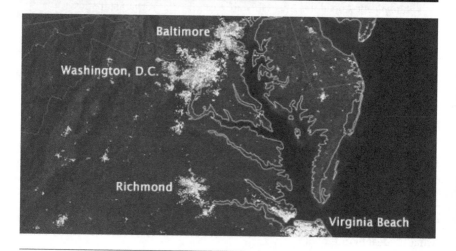

Source: NASA, "NOAA/NASA Satellite Sees Holiday Lights Brighten Cities" (December 16, 2014), http://www.nasa.gov/content/goddard/satellite-sees-holiday-lights-brighten-cities.

then we'll have to do more than just use energy-efficient cars and appliances," Roman told a reporter. "We also need to understand how dominant social phenomena, the changing demographics of urban centers, and socio-cultural settings affect energy-use decisions."[13]

It was a great holiday story that was picked up by media across the country. The story was in part about the Earth-based exploits of genuine rocket scientists producing incredibly interesting photos. The holiday photos gave NASA a chance to compare other human impacts on the environment in other countries around other religious holidays. It provided an opportunity to dig deeper into the agency's basic research on assessing the impact of greenhouse gases on energy production and how to measure the impact that alternative lighting systems might have on energy use and greenhouse gas production. It proved a great example of how anecdotes and stories can cascade into much bigger issues and support a far more nuanced discussion of important ideas.

Not all stories, of course, are as good or as based in fact as is NASA's tale of holiday lights in the eastern United States. Sorting out valid from phony tales is a tough job, especially since some false tales can seem ultra-believable or, like the effect of bone marrow treatment on breast cancer, can be stories we *want* to believe. But at the bottom of the debate about anecdotes, two points emerge clearly. One is that, whether analysts like it or not, anecdotes will always be more powerful in policy debates than are thick piles of peer-reviewed analyses. The other is that, since anecdotes are so powerful, it makes a lot of sense to figure out how to produce *good* tales—and sniff out the bad ones.

Mediating Information

None of this, however, happens easily or naturally. Not only don't data speak for themselves. Those who do sophisticated data analysis often speak in a language that's hard to translate for nonprofessionals. Means, medians, variance, regression, t-tests, and other significance tests typically don't connect well with audiences who often reach just for "the average." Policymakers typically wonder whether a new idea is going to work or what can be done to fix an old one. Analysts are from Mars, policymakers are from Venus, and there's a big distance in between. Connecting policy decisions with the best evidence requires a very sophisticated bridge.

Selling the story thus needs a three-way link. There is the *supply side:* the information, data, and evidence that analysts have. A data dump on policymakers rarely works, since they rarely have the training to interpret the information on their own, the time to do so, or the inclination to invest effort in a process without an obvious payoff. So analysts need to figure out how to present their evidence in a way that policymakers will *want* it and *use* it.

Then there's the *demand side:* the information that policymakers would *like* to have (or might be persuaded to use) before setting or changing course. Analysts often forget that, no matter how powerful they think their analyses might be, policymakers don't really *need* the analysis before making a decision. So policymakers need to *see* the value of evidence that's available and *want* to reach out for it.

Finally, there's the *bridge:* the intermediaries who make the supply-demand connection. There are supply and demand forces in the marketplace, of course, but most of the time they don't meet spontaneously. Making deals between buyers and sellers requires a marketplace. Farmers growing produce and consumers who want the freshest tomatoes can't count on bumping into each other on the street. Instead, they rely on markets, whether an enormous supermarket or a small farmer's market. Hungry diners and chefs need a place to exchange money for delicious food, whether it's a five-star restaurant or a food truck. Students buying books need a way to connect with publishers, whether it's a campus bookstore or an online retailer like Amazon. And Amazon itself needs intermediaries, including the Internet and delivery systems, such as UPS, FedEx, and its own trucks and planes.

For policymakers and analysts to connect, they typically need intermediaries: individual staff members who can make the links or, sometimes, whole offices devoted to helping tell and sell the story of evidence so policymakers can know better what they should do. And the most important job that intermediaries can perform is connecting evidence, which is often broad and rooted in academic study to the problems to be solved—and connecting the problems, which are often complex and dynamic, to the evidence that can help solve them. As the U.S. Office of Management and Budget (OMB) argued in its 2017 analytical documents, "Evidence cannot be separated from the purposes for which it is being used, and the credible use of evidence in decision-making requires an under-standing of what conclusions can and, equally important, cannot be drawn from the information."[14]

One especially tough issue that attracted an effort to bridge supply and demand of data is student debt. The debt facing students entering the job mar-ket, when they need to begin repaying their loans, resumed its upward climb following the 2008 economic crisis (see Figure 4.4). As college costs increase and the struggle to find good jobs grows, the debt burden of college graduates has become a bigger issue for young Americans and their families. Some critics wonder whether college is worth it. And for federal policymakers facing rising deficits and a growing national debt, the rising student loan burden has framed tough questions about how much aid, in which forms, the federal government ought to provide.

To get at these questions, the Obama administration created a College Scorecard, which provides students and their parents with information on how much colleges cost, what their graduation rates are, how much debt students accumulate, and what post-college earnings have been. That, OMB argues, "enable[s] them to make better informed choices about colleges that fit their educational and career aspirations."[15] In addition, the College Scorecard pro-vides an open dataset that permits researchers to explore other issues that could help families make the best college choices. The College Scorecard brings

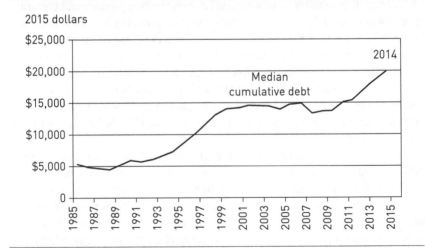

FIGURE 4.4 • Rising Levels of Student Loan Debt

2015 dollars

Source: Council of Economic Advisers, *Investing in Higher Education: Benefits, Challenges, and the State of Student Debt* (July 2016), 26, https://www.whitehouse.gov/sites/default/files/page/files/20160718_cea_student_debt.pdf.

together data from the Department of Education, especially on college loans and college performance, to tax data collected by the Department of Transportation. Neither department has *all* the information needed to put together a complete picture, but together their intermediaries have packaged the data in a way that helps students sort out the questions they most need to answer: How much will college really cost, and is it worth it? It also helps policymakers determine how best to improve support for college students to relieve the enormous burdens students often face.

The College Scorecard website (https://collegescorecard.ed.gov) offers links to schools with low costs that lead to high incomes, among other data (see Figure 4.5). It gives students and their families information about loans and grants to pay for colleges and provides fascinating factoids:

- College graduates, on average, earn $1 million more over their lifetimes than individuals with only a high school education.
- Some students are eligible for $5,775 in free Pell grants to pay for college, and the grants don't have to be repaid.
- Thirty percent of college students began college at age twenty-five or older.

Students can use the website to find schools that best fit them, based on the programs they offer, their location, and their size.

Inside this website, however, is an enormous amount of background data, including information on the rising debt levels that many college students face. Analysts can read the policy and technical papers that the website provides—and download an enormous amount of data (more than 212 megabytes as of March 2016; all 363 pages of OMB's historical tables on the federal budget amount to just 1.8 megabytes of data). And since the data are "open"—available to anyone—any analyst anywhere can sort through the evidence to examine any question in whatever way seems to make sense. The data are richly detailed and come from several

FIGURE 4.5 • College Scorecard from the U.S. Department of Education

Check Out These Schools

23 four-year schools with **low costs that lead to high incomes**

By state, two-year colleges where students earn **high salaries after graduation**

30 four-year schools with **high graduation rates and low costs**

15 public four-year colleges with **high graduation leading to high incomes**

Source: U.S. Department of Education, "College Scorecard," https://collegescorecard.ed.gov.

datasets. And they can lead to some especially intricate models, as the formula for allocating state aid to Tennessee's four-year colleges shows (see Figure 4.6).

The data, moreover, have led to some sharp comparisons and fierce debates among some of the schools. For example, the College Scorecard project found that, for the lowest-income students, the "net price"—what students actually pay—at Columbia University was much lower than at New York University. Columbia graduates had lower debt, higher rates of completion, and substantially higher income (see Figure 4.7). The Department of Education did not criticize either university and pointed out that specific programs at the different universities might be a better fit depending on the student. But putting the data out stimulated a very fundamental national debate, among students, parents,

---

FIGURE 4.6 • Tennessee's Outcome-Based Funding Formula for Four-Year Colleges

$$F = \left[w_{H24} \left(H24 + 0.4H24_A + 0.4H24_p \right) + w_{H48} \left(H48 + 0.4H48_A + 0.4H48_p \right) + \right.$$

$$w_{H72} \left(H72 + 0.4H72_A + 0.4H72_p \right) + w_D \left(D + 0.4D_A + 0.4DP \right) + \frac{w_M M}{0.3} +$$

$$\left. \frac{w_L L}{0.05} + \frac{w_R R}{20.000} + w_T T + \frac{w_Q Q}{0.02} + \frac{w_G G}{0.04} \right] \times s$$

Source: U.S. Department of Education, *Using Federal Data to Measure and Improve the Performance of U.S. Institutions of Higher Education* (September 2015), 17, https://collegescorecard.ed.gov/assets/UsingFederalDataToMeasureAndImprovePerformance.pdf.

FIGURE 4.7 • Data on Columbia University and New York University

	Net price for the lowest-income students	Median loan debt of completers	Completion rate	Median earnings
Columbia University	$8,086	$19,435	94%	$73,000
NYU	$25,441	$23,250	84%	$58,800

Source: U.S. Department of Education, *Better Information for Better College Choice and Institutional Performance* (September 2015), 13, https://collegescorecard.ed.gov/assets/BetterInformationForBetterCollegeChoiceAndInstitutionalPerformance.pdf.

college officials, and policymakers, about how best to deal with the rising tide of student loan debt in the country.

Students and their parents want information about whether their investment in college pays off—and where it's most likely to benefit them. Colleges and universities are under big pressure to control their costs and improve their products. The federal government is providing billions of dollars of support in grants and loans. Everyone wants to find ways of improving the value of college. These data have stimulated and sharpened the debate, not only because of the analyses that the Department of Education has produced but also through the open data, which make it possible for other analysts to do their own digging. There's a big supply of data in the Treasury and Department of Education archives. There's a huge demand among all the players. The Department of Education's College Scorecard project created the intermediary to bring it all together.

Making the Sale

Selling the data story requires several interlocking pieces: connecting the problems that policymakers need to solve with evidence that analysts can use to help solve them, in a language that helps policymakers understand solutions and analysts stay true to the validity of their analyses. Analyses often fail because analysts dump the data and assume that policymakers will see in it what they see. Policymakers often fail to pick up the data because they face enormous piles of information, in an arcane language, which sometimes conflict and rarely speak to them clearly. And citizens—well, citizens often emerge from data discussions with great cynicism, assuming that all the players are spinning the numbers to fit their own point of view and that, as civilians, they can't make sense of complicated data to begin with.

This is often a source of enormous frustration for analysts, who devote their careers to trying to understand complex phenomena and write papers that pass the tests of their colleagues and that focus on really important questions. When policymakers fail to pick up and act on what analysts say, they blame the policymakers in particular and the system more generally. They rarely look to themselves or to the need to find the intermediary who can translate their findings into actionable intelligence on which policymakers want to take action. And they often find themselves tempted, as we'll see in the next chapter, to sell what partisans in the process want to buy. That not only raises big questions of ethics but also deepens the cynicism that many players have anyway.

As we've seen in this chapter, this isn't an impossible dilemma. It's possible to sell even the most complex data, including rocket science, if it's done in thoughtful and clever ways. But it requires a high level of attention to the basic challenge of language and to building a marketplace of ideas in which buyers and sellers can find common language and common ground. And it's possible to make even the simplest issues too muddy to see, if analysts forget that one of their most important jobs is creating a language to communicate clearly the messages they want to send.

Building this marketplace and speaking above the noise in the political system, however, is challenging. Fortunately, as we'll see in Chapter 5, there are solutions.

Notes

1. Clive Thompson, "PowerPoint Makes You Dumb," *New York Times* (December 14, 2003), http://www.nytimes.com/2003/12/14/magazine/14POWER.html.

2. *Columbia* Accident Investigation Board, *Report Volume 1* (Washington, DC: Government Printing Office, 2003), 191, http://s3.amazonaws.com/akamai.netstorage/anon.nasa-global/CAIB/CAIB_medres_full.pdf.

3. Noah Shachtman, "Military Faces Bandwidth Crunch," *Wired* (January 31, 2003), http://archive.wired.com/techbiz/it/news/2003/01/57420; see also Richard Stiennon, "How PowerPoint Kicked Off a Revolution in Military Affairs," *Forbes*, http://www.forbes.com/sites/richardstiennon/2015/07/20/how-power-point-kicked-off-rma/#1fc6a1ca6a40.

4. Edward R. Tufte, "PowerPoint and Military Intelligence," http://www.edwardtufte.com/bboard/q-and-a-fetch-msg?msg_id=0000fv. More broadly, for a piercing critique of the use of PowerPoint, see Edward R. Tufte, *The Cognitive Style of PowerPoint: Pitching out Corrupts within,* 2nd ed. (Cheshire, CT: Graphics Press, 2006).

5. "Self-Deprecating Bush Talks to Yale Grads," Fox News (May 21, 2001), http://www.foxnews.com/story/2001/05/21/self-deprecating-bush-talks-to-yale-grads.html; and Dean Obeidallah, "How Obama Has Weaponized Wit," CNN (March 21, 2013), http://www.cnn.com/2013/03/21/opinion/obeidallah-presidential-jokes.

6. Judi Atkins and Alan Finlayson, "'. . . A 40-Year-Old Black Man Made the Point to Me': Everyday Knowledge and the Performance of Leadership in Contemporary British Politics," *Political Studies* 61 (2012), 161–167; Justin Parkinson, "Are Politicians Too Obsessed with Anecdotes?," BBC News (January 30, 2013), http://www.bbc.com/news/uk-politics-20956126.

7. Matthew Dowd, "The Allure of an Anecdote," ABC News (October 29, 2013), http://abcnews.go.com/Politics/allure-anecdote/story?id=20719195.

8. "State and Local Perspectives on the Impact of the Data Explosion," *Government Business Council* (July 2016), http://m.govexec.com/insights/flash-poll-series-data-management/?oref=NL.

9. Diana Furchtgott-Roth and Jared Meyer, "Obamacare Is a Horror Story for Young Americans," *National Review* (May 19, 2015), http://www.nationalreview.com/article/418322/obamacare-horror-story-young-americans-diana-furchtgott-roth-jared-meyer.

10. John E. McDonough, "Using and Misusing Anecdote in Policy Making," *Health Affairs,* 20 (January 2001), 207–212, http://content.healthaffairs.org/content/20/1/207.full.

11. Stephen Jay Gould, *Bully for Brontosaurus: Reflections in* *Natural History* (New York: W. W. Norton, 1992), 251.

12. Deborah A. Stone, *Policy Paradox: The Art of Political Decision Making,* 3rd ed. (New York: W. W. Norton, 2012).

13. Ed Mazza, "Christmas Lights Can Be Seen from Space by NASA Satellites," *Huffington Post* (December 17, 2014), http://www.huffingtonpost.com/2014/12/17/christmas-lights-seen-from-space_n_6338578.html.

14. U.S. Office of Management and Budget, "Building the Capacity to Produce and Use Evidence," in *Budget of the United States, Fiscal Year 2017: Analytical Perspectives* (Washington, DC: 2016), 69, https://www.gpo.gov/fdsys/pkg/BUDGET-2017-PER/pdf/BUDGET-2017-PER-4-3.pdf.

15. Ibid., 75.

Speak above the Noise

N o one really knows how many Americans suffer from gephyrophobia. You might not know the word, but the odds are good that you or a friend has acquaintance with it: a fear of bridges. Many a driver has suffered the quivering feeling in the pit of the stomach and the sweating of the palms that comes from driving a car over a long bridge ten stories or more over a deep body of water. Some gephyrophobics will drive hours out of their way to avoid long bridges. For governments running the bridges, gephyrophobia can be a major problem, when panicked drivers simply stop their cars in the middle of busy bridges. There are several pay-to-drive services for travelers who don't want to white-knuckle their way across the Chesapeake Bay Bridge (over four miles long and eighteen stories above the water at its highest point), usually listed among the nation's scariest bridges. For Michigan's Mackinac Bridge (almost five miles long and about twenty stories above the water, between the state's upper and lower peninsulas), the state offers a free drive-across service—drivers only have to pull over and use a phone box on either side of the bridge.

So if you're a gephyrophobic, you won't want to read what follows. Bridges don't last forever and, in fact, Michigan's highway department says, "Bridges are typically designed to provide 30 years of service."[1] The Mackinac Bridge has been exceptionally well maintained, and it celebrated its fifty-eighth birthday in 2016. For the bridge's engineers, keeping the bridge in good shape means knowing its condition—and points of particular stress—before little problems become big ones. To get a good fix on how the bridge is coping with the enormous stresses of wind, temperature changes, and traffic, a bold Michigan State University professor, Nizar Lajnef, was lowered over the side to install stress sensors on the bridge.

The sensors are clever devices; they get their power from the energy generated by movement across the bridge, and they transmit their data wirelessly back to the data collection point. The price when in full production: just $1 each. Looking forward to his trip over the side, dangling hundreds of feet over the water, Lajnef said, "I think it will be fun"—as long as he could avoid vertigo.[2]

Lajnef's sensors are part of a far broader movement called the *Internet of things*—a step past using the Internet to share information to using it to monitor and control objects. Not only is it possible to use a smartphone as a remote control for televisions and video recorders. Consumers can buy "smart thermostats" to control the temperature in their homes, even if they're on the other side of the world. They can start their cars remotely or use their smartphones to manage vacuums that clean their floors. They can buy devices that sit happily on a shelf, talk to them, and ask them to do things ranging from turning on lights to answering homework questions. Along with the rest of society, governments have aggressively moved into the Internet of things. For example, governments are using the Internet to track garbage collection and map, in real time, the best collection routes, as some trucks fill up and others can switch routes. In the Netherlands, smart garbage bins fitted with chips help managers predict when the bins are getting full. That avoids spending money to collect garbage when bins are mostly empty or causing inconvenience if they wait until they're overflowing to empty them. Analysts estimated that the government was saving about 20 percent of its operating costs by using fewer vehicles, traveling fewer miles, and emitting less pollution.[3] The Internet of things, however, is also capable of causing almost unimaginable mischief. In October 2016, hackers launched an attack using digital video recorders and cameras that crippled Netflix, Twitter, and PayPal, among other websites. We've reached the point where someone in a basement can attack an Xbox or a nanny cam and cripple the Internet, because so many of our devices are interconnected—and the interconnections create a highway for electronic sabotage.

Beyond the Internet of things, some governments are experimenting with new ways of using technology to engage citizens. Mayor Chris Cabaldon (D-West Sacramento, CA) explained that his city was using a variant of the dating app Tinder to give citizens a chance to weigh in on different policy choices—swipe right to "like" a two-story apartment building, low-rise with less density, or swipe left to "like" a design for a five-story apartment building with a café on the first floor, because the larger building creates more traffic.[4]

Then there's the use of *predictive analytics* to help solve the problem of tensions between police officers and their communities. In Baltimore, for example, a police officer charged with shooting at a car driving toward him had previously been implicated in two other shootings. In addition, the officer had a history of citizen complaints, for both excessive force and harassment. The U.S. Justice Department concluded that the Baltimore police department "failed to respond to those alerts in a way that could have uncovered the officer's condition or otherwise allowed for an intervention."[5] Police departments are developing early-intervention systems to mine the data collected on individual officers' behavior, identify signs of potential future problems, and intervene before the smaller issues spark major crises.

"The idea is to take the data from these police departments and help them predict which officers are at risk of these adverse incidents," explained Rayid Ghani, a data scientist at the University of Chicago. "Can I detect these things early? And if I can detect them early, can I direct intervention to them—training, counseling?" The goal: create algorithms that explore data that the police department already has, identify potential problems, filter out the inevitable bias that comes from a system based on complaints, and develop a strategy to make better predictions about future problems—and develop the most effective interventions. The strategy, Ghani explained, can be used on a host of local issues, from helping Cincinnati determine from past experience just what emergency medical service equipment to dispatch in responding to a call, to helping Syracuse decide where best to invest its maintenance budget on the city's water mains. "What we believe," Ghani said, "is the role of data analytics is to help do a lot of early warning systems, to help do a lot of preventative things, to help allocate resources more effectively, and to sort of help improve policy in a much more evidence-based way than we've been doing before."[6]

Local governments are using data analytics to decide how to deal with calls for suspected child abuse. Counties bear most of that responsibility, and no county has a large enough staff to answer all the calls. On the other hand, missing one of the calls could put a child in serious jeopardy. "It's just a tremendous amount of volume, so you can imagine how quickly those decisions have to be made," explained Erin Dalton of the Allegheny County, Pennsylvania, Department of Human Services. In addition to looking at a family's history, the county relies on a data tool that digs information out of its data warehouse, which contains more than a billion records. The warehouse produces a *family screen score* for households. The higher the score, the greater the odds of a problem. "If we can do something that's going to improve our decision making, that's worth it," explained the county's human services director Marc Cherna. "Especially on this front-end piece, because it can save children's lives." But this use of data analytics also brings big risks, because it "magnifies all the bias that's already built into child welfare and is extremely dangerous," said Richard Wexler, executive director of the National Coalition for Child Protection Reform. Some of these systems, he said, risk increasing problems of racial bias.[7]

How to Know What We Know

Smarter devices—and smarter analysts—unquestionably are opening more doors to help us know what best to do. But the rise of technology also raises a host of big problems. Figuring out what we know requires working through five issues.

Humility

Let's begin by revisiting an important lesson from Chapter 1: decision makers just don't *need* analysts to tell them what they should do. There's a powerful grounding that comes from the electoral process. Politicians have gone before the people, made their case, and collected enough votes to win office. There's nothing quite like standing in front of a crowd, making the case, getting an enthusiastic response, and using that to build confidence in a policy idea. All of that can happen with powerful rhetoric and a smartphone's Twitter app. It surely can occur without policy analysis, a thick policy playbook, detailed plans, or even many specific proposals. When Donald Trump rode the escalator to the lobby of his Fifth Avenue tower in June 2015 to launch his presidential campaign, most prognosticators viewed it as just another episode in a reality show. Yet he dispatched sixteen opponents to win the Republican presidential nomination, and with a staff of seventy—just one-tenth of what Hillary Clinton put together in her winning nomination campaign. He had no pollsters for much of the time and often pulled together his speeches on the fly, sometimes on his plane's final approach to the airport in the town hosting a campaign rally. No one—perhaps not even Trump himself—imagined that he could ride this strategy to victory.

Policy analysts need to begin with a large helping of humility. Politicians just don't need them. That's not to say that policy decisions in particular, and the world in general, wouldn't be better if we knew more and relied on that knowledge to do better. Alice Rivlin—whose career has taken her from a top position in Lyndon B. Johnson's War on Poverty, to a job as founding director of the U.S. Congressional Budget Office, to the top job at the U.S. Office of Management and Budget, and to the number-two job at the Federal Reserve—started her career as an eager analyst, convinced about the "enormous potential for progress in reducing poverty, increasing the effectiveness of education for low-income children, and improving health services—if only we did the right things. Alas, the problems have proved more intractable than a young enthusiast imagined."[8]

Rivlin's wise words provide a dose of reality for enthusiastic efforts to know better and do better. Problems often turn out to be more complicated than they seem. Answers are often harder to come by than analysts imagine. Policymakers are perfectly capable of latching on to big ideas—whether the War on Poverty on the left or school choice on the right—because, well, they just seem like the right things to do. Their campaign experience tells them that they're right, even if the analysis doesn't always agree. For their part, as we'll see, analysts can never really be sure they're right.

So, when it's time to decide, decision makers often put their finger to the wind and choose the path that seems right, whether they have analytic backup or not. Analysts therefore need to begin their work with a heavy dose of humility. Their work is invaluable. But, to be frank, decision makers don't really need them. A quip by Ted Turner, who founded CNN, makes the point. "If I only had a little humility, I'd be perfect," he said.[9]

Uncertainty

More humility leads to a better understanding of uncertainty, especially what they know they don't know—and what they don't know they don't know. Analysts seek to know the answers to important questions, but it's often the case that the more important the question, the less certain the answer. What causes poverty, and how can we cure it? How can we deal with income inequality? Even more straightforward questions don't have certain answers. For example, what's the best way to plow snow? On January 21, 2016, for example, the Washington, D.C., area received about an inch of snow. Snow-savvy Midwesterners laughed at the result: thousands of drivers got stuck for hours. Trips that usually take less than an hour stalled drivers on highways for nine hours or more. Some drivers told their friends the next day that they had the chance to catch up on episodes of *Game of Thrones* on their smartphones while stuck in traffic. Others didn't make it home until 3:00 a.m. Even President Obama, on his way back from a day trip to Detroit, found himself jammed in traffic. The president usually rode a helicopter back to the White House. The storm made that impossible, so he had to use a motorcade. Despite flashing lights and sirens, a drive that usually takes thirty minutes stretched to seventy-four minutes, with the president's car skidding perilously close to accidents along the way.[10] One driver said the response was "pathetic." Washington mayor Muriel Bowser apologized and called the city's response "inadequate."[11]

The cause of the chaos? It's not that forecasters didn't see the storm coming. They predicted a light dusting—but they were concentrating instead on the forecast of a monster storm that seemed to be heading their way a few days later. Highway officials didn't think that an inch of snow would cause much trouble, so they didn't pretreat the roads. Temperatures hovered around freezing, and the traffic packed the snow into a sheet of ice. It began around rush hour, so once the traffic got backed up it was impossible to get equipment to the worst areas because the traffic was already stuck. Uncertainty about the effects of an inch of snow, with forecasters and transportation officials looking down the road at another storm, caused chaos that reached to the White House.

The lessons here are important. First, *we can't know everything*. It's not that computer models didn't predict that the flakes were coming. It's that the experts didn't think that such a tiny amount of snow would cause such chaos. Washington drivers are notorious for not knowing how to drive in snow and panicking at the first flake. But after such misadventures, who could blame them? With dense traffic around the Capitol, even tiny problems can cause big delays. A light snowfall that Midwesterners would laugh off can become a major crisis, especially because winter temperatures often hover right at freezing and turn a small amount of snow into an unnavigable glaze of ice.

Second, *we can't be sure of what we do know*. Road engineers have invented a technique of spraying roadways with beet juice before storms, which keeps the road from icing in the early hours of a storm. But they didn't think they needed to do it in this case. Based on their experience, they thought the chances of problems were slim. They're usually very good—but they missed it this time.

Third, *we sometimes know the wrong things.* The big storm on the way didn't disappoint. The day before the January 21 mini-storm, forecasters were looking at a "massive snowstorm" that was likely to occur two days later and predicted it would produce twelve to twenty inches in the Washington area.[12] It came, on time, and it was massive—even bigger than the forecasters expected. In downtown Washington, snow totals reached eighteen to twenty-four inches, a monster storm even for snow-savvy Midwesterners. The forecasters nailed the timing but underestimated its size. But by looking ahead at the really big storm coming, they missed the tiny one that arrived first and caused such chaos.

Fourth, *some of what we know conflicts with other things we know.* The D.C. metropolitan area highway departments have highly skilled experts who understand the region, its weather, and its tangled network of roads. Their usual assumption is that it's not worth deploying a lot of equipment for small snowfalls of an inch or so. They have concluded that's too little to plow and it's not worth spending money to spread chemicals, because heavy traffic usually melts the snow. Their experience told them it was better to focus on the coming mega-storm. The phone calls they got from furious motorists, some of whom it took four hours to go half a mile, told them otherwise.

Policy analysts spend much of their time determining how best to deal with uncertainty. They begin by assuming that it's hard to know what numbers to trust. They know they need to exercise great care in connecting one set of numbers (like the benefits provided to poor families) with another (like the likelihood workers in these families will leave welfare for paying jobs). And they are very careful in asserting causality: that a policy change produces specific outcomes. This is the core of the statistical analysis that lies at the core of efforts to know how best to solve policy problems—and it's all about managing uncertainty.

Behind these statistical questions, however, are the puzzles framed by Washington's nasty brush with an inch of snow. How can public officials deal with the enormous uncertainties that often come along with even the most straightforward policy puzzles?

Equity

The path to knowing, moreover, doesn't treat everyone equally. Part of the problem is access. The more we rely on technology to connect citizens with government, the more equal treatment of citizens depends on access to the technology. Access to the Internet is vastly better now than in its early days, when it was mainly a domain for the well-to-do and where there were enormous pricing differences between quick, easy connections and slow, barely usable ones. Most schools now have access to high-speed Internet service, and 70 percent of adults have broadband access at home, according to a 2013 survey by the Pew Research Center. Internet access, however, varies greatly:

- *By education.* Among those with at least a college degree, 89 percent have broadband access. For those without a high school diploma, it's 37 percent.
- *By race and ethnicity.* Among whites, 74 percent have access. Among blacks, it's 64 percent, and for Hispanics, it's 53 percent.
- *By income.* It's no surprise that 88 percent of families making more than $75,000 a year have broadband. For those making less than $30,000, it's 54 percent.
- *By urban/suburban/rural split.* Suburbanites have the most access, at 73 percent. For city dwellers, it's 70 percent, compared with 62 percent for those in rural areas.[13]

The spread of smartphones offers hope in closing the gap. Pew found that 56 percent of Americans own a smartphone, and 10 percent have a smartphone but no Internet connection. That means that, through their mobile phone provider, they can connect to the Internet even if they don't have broadband at home. That's especially important for blacks and Latinos. Pew found that the use of smartphones almost eliminates the broadband gap. But 20 percent of Americans have neither—and thus have no personal access to the rapidly growing world of the Web and government's efforts to connect with them through it.[14] Technology gaps are gradually shrinking as smartphones and broadband become more universal. But these gaps haven't disappeared. Strategies of knowing—and methods of connecting government with citizens—still need to work on the assumption that the Internet isn't yet an equal tool.

Beyond the challenge of equity in access is the effect of the use of data on equality. Cathy O'Neil, who writes a blog called Mathbabe, has highlighted what she calls "creepy models" of data analysis, especially in "big data." She points to one company that provides employers with predictions, based on publicly available data, that forecast which of their employees are most likely to leave the company. She highlighted another company's efforts to predict the outcome of litigation based on artificial intelligence. "What could possibly go wrong?" she asked.[15] The answer: what she calls "weapons of math destruction," in which carefully drawn statistical models produce important conclusions that, in fact, build on fallible—and sometimes incorrect—assumptions.[16]

Data analysis and, she argues, big data can aggravate inequality. She points to models of recidivism, which predict the criminals most likely to repeat their crimes. "People are being labeled high risk by the models because they live in poor neighborhoods and therefore, they're being sentenced longer," she argues. "That exacerbates that cycle." And, she says, it reinforces the behavior of police in ways that increase tensions with poor neighborhoods.[17]

Not only can such data analysis disadvantage the poor. O'Neil contends it can also hurt women in the workplace. She points to one San Francisco–based startup company, which quantified an applicant's social capital to help in hiring decisions. Part of the score was based on whether applicants visited a Japanese manga website, which featured comics. The problem, she said, was that many women didn't visit the site because they found the sexual tone of the sites offensive. As a result, female applicants were being hurt in the scoring process. And, she went on:

> An engineering firm wants to hire an engineer, but in order to build an algorithm to help it, it needs to define success. It defines success with historical data as someone who has been there for two years and has been promoted at least once. The historical data says no woman has ever been here for two years and been promoted, so then the algorithm learns that women will never succeed.

Using the past to make decisions about the future can thus become a self-fulfilling prophecy. "If we hand over our decision-making processes to computers that use historical data, it will just repeat history," she argues. "And that simply is not okay."[18]

Data, especially big data, can help us know a great deal we did not know before. But sometimes the sources from which the data come introduce bias, like who reads which online comics. Sometimes the ways in which the data are processed introduce bias, like building predictive models that favor some individuals over others.

Smart analysts often think they can avoid such issues in equity, but the problem is much tougher than it often appears. The inherent biases can sometimes be deceptively hard to spot. Polls that rely on Internet or phone surveys inevitably bring some individuals in and leave others out. Some data can be the product of policies that themselves might reflect bias, like racial profiling in police departments.

Moreover, such problems are impossible to avoid. It's impossible to know everything about anything. The more complex a problem and the bigger the supply of data, the more decisions analysts need to make about where to focus their energy. Every step that brings some information in and leaves other information out inevitably involves judgments: which issues matter most and which ones can be left on the side. Analysts can't work without filtering, and every filtering decision is based on values. Values almost always introduce biases, sometimes known but often unseen. Big data opens up many new doors. But it also frames lots of big new problems.

So no analyst can ever hope to produce "value-free" analysis. But every good analyst can look carefully at the values that shape the analysis—and be transparent about what drives it as well as what gets left out.

Ethics

Since values are central to analysis, it's always tempting to twist the analysis to fit the values. Clever analysts can take most issues and produce a case for almost any perspective—and many analysts do. Focus on some assumptions here, emphasize some data there, and it's possible to put together a case for the decision that an interest group wants to advance. Moreover, analysis is never free. Someone has to pay analysts to collect the data, analyze it, write the reports, prepare the PowerPoint slides, meet quietly with allies, craft press releases, build convincing charts, and do all the things that make analysis powerful. Analysts usually know who's paying the bills. That tells them what the preferred conclusion is, and it can be very, very tempting for analysts to provide ammunition for the perspectives they know the funder wants to advance—especially if the funder is also the analyst's employer, since there might be an unspoken message that continued work and promotions depend on coming up with the "right answer" to the problem. It's one thing to launch a bold quest for the right answer to a tough problem. It's often more complicated when an analyst launches that quest with rent to pay, a baby to feed, and student loans to repay—and the analyst knows what answer the employer wants.

In looking at the same data in the federal budget, analysts working for the Heritage Foundation, which advances conservative perspectives, and analysts employed by the Progressive Policy Institute, which leans left, often look at the same numbers and produce different conclusions. At the state level, the right-leaning American Legislative Exchange Council often ends up in a different place than the Sierra Club. There are often fierce battles between analysts working for labor and for industry, between those worried about climate change and those concerned about job development, between interests representing the defense industry and those arguing for a cutback in the nation's military posture.

It's certainly not true that every analysis reflects the perspective of the organization funding it, or that analysts simply gin up whatever they know the funder wants. Most organizations are full of analysts sharing similar perspectives, so it's not surprising that they end up in similar places. No one would want—or get—or keep—a job working for people with whom they strongly disagree. The World Wildlife Fund attracts people interested in protecting animals. Local chambers of commerce lure people who want to help businesses grow. Groupthink, in fact, can filter the way analysts see problems, what information they trust the most, what assumptions make the most sense, and what conclusions they draw.[19]

It's not *always* the case that analysts work within such tight boundaries. Sometimes funders want new, original thinking and are happy for analysts to take the information wherever it leads them. Sometimes funders don't know what they want and are glad to give analysts a wide lane in which to drive, in the hope of coming up with breakthrough ideas. But, often, information emerges from organizations with known or predictable points of view. What is the obligation of analysts: to give those paying the bills what they want or to provide the analysts' best judgment even it doesn't match what funders want? Idealists typically answer that analysts should go where the data lead them, but in reality it can be a tough dilemma. In the first case, analysts might have to push some data aside and bring other assumptions in so as to provide what the funder wants, and that can make analysts feel smarmy. In the second case, analysts know that if they produce the "wrong" conclusion they might not have a job for long. The fundamental ethical questions are often sharp and serious.

So what's an analyst to do, especially when the economic implications, including earning enough money to make the mortgage, car, and day care payments, are large? Analysts, of course, have to look into the mirror and be able to live with themselves. They have their own values that frame their internal compasses. They often share values with those in the organizations for which they work. Those all provide important cues.

But there's also an important additional contribution that analysts can make. Even though analysts might know the conclusions their bosses want, there's always a hidden puzzle: What is lurking out there that might surprise me—and my funder? Sometimes the analyst's biggest contribution lies in pointing out clearly, at least inside the organization, the assumptions and potential trouble spots that could undermine the conclusions they've reached. How would an opponent seek to destroy the analysis an organization produces? Even if an organization begins by knowing where it wants to come out, and even if analysts know it's their job to produce the ammunition to support it, they can provide enormous value by identifying the tripwires that could undercut that conclusion.

The leader of a major Washington interest group once told me that his most valuable analysts were not those with the best technical statistical skills. Rather, he said, he greatly appreciated those who knew how to look at a study and challenge it, even if the study were one that his own organization was producing. He told me about the email he got late at night from one very excited analyst. She had been working for weeks to understand how an opposing interest group had produced what seemed to be a very powerful study that came to the opposite conclusion of his own organization. "I finally figured it out!" she said. She went on to explain how one of the assumptions in their opponent's work could—and should—be challenged. And, in pulling that assumption out, the other group's conclusions collapsed like a game of Jenga.

Analysts have an ethical responsibility to their own values. They have an ethical obligation not to undermine those for whom they're working. But that doesn't mean that they should blindly chase after predetermined conclusions. They need to understand, clearly and fully, the value implications of the crucial decisions they make in conducting their analysis—precisely where an assumption here or a statistical test there might nudge their analysis toward a value-laden conclusion. And they can contribute great value by helping their own organization understand how others in the game of analysis are doing the same, whether intentionally or not.

No boss wants to be surprised to find the organization's analysis torpedoed by another interest that discovers an unexplored vulnerability. And every boss quietly smiles when the organization's analysts are able to find vulnerabilities in another group's findings. The conclusion: don't tell 'em what they want; tell 'em what they'll wish they knew, before they're surprised that they don't know it.

The answer to these tough dilemmas isn't to try to be unbiased. That's impossible. Rather, it's to shine a bright light on the way that values shape the outcomes. It's transparency, not impartiality, that's key. That's the height of ethical behavior in complex and contentious battles.

Privacy

But if transparency lies at the core of so many challenges of knowing, how should we deal with the imperative of privacy? Knowing more always risks knowing too much, especially about things that individuals wish they could keep secret. That's a problem that many smartphone and Facebook users wish they had discovered sooner. Once they push information out into the Internet, it's almost impossible to get it back. And once it's out there, it's impossible to control what anyone does with it: from a photo shared a bit too casually to personal information stolen from a government website.

The dilemmas are growing exponentially with the information revolution, with the rise of big data, and with government's increasing use of information to guide policy decisions. One part of the problem is protecting the information that government collects. Cyberthieves, widely suspected to be from China, stole the personal information of more than twenty-five million current and former government employees and members of their families. The U.S. Office of Personnel Management had collected the information as part of the employment and background check process and it failed to protect the system against intruders, who made off with information about individuals ranging from members of Congress to the children of government workers.

Snowden, a 2016 film about Edward Snowden and his decision to leak information about the National Security Agency's (NSA) collection of data on Americans' phone calls, stimulated a fierce debate. The NSA had not vacuumed up information about individual calls but rather tracked metadata about who was calling whom, as part of an effort to track terrorists who might be using mobile phones to plot attacks. Snowden stole the data from the government and his employer, Booz Allen Hamilton, and he leaked it to reporters, who published stories in London's *The Guardian* newspaper and in the *Washington Post.* (In a sign of just how complex the issue was, the NSA is based in Ft. Meade, Maryland, not far from Washington, D.C. Snowden was working on government projects as an employee of the private contractor, Booz Allen, but he did his work in Hawaii. To get access to the information, he needed a government security clearance, which was processed by yet another private contractor. The metadata on which he was working came from NSA's collection of information about phone calls made through private phone companies. This tangled tale demonstrates just how hard it is to define—and resolve—the ethical issues that lie at the core of so many big policy puzzles.) Some people hailed Snowden as a hero for exposing the vast array of government snooping. Some condemned him as a traitor for breaking his oath of secrecy and exposing the government's intelligence collection systems. And some believed both points. All these positions revolved around issues of privacy.

Even the rising importance of the Internet of things raises important privacy questions. Tracking local government garbage trucks and snow plows as they work the streets is one thing. But some citizens get queasy at the idea that government is using Internet-of-things technology, through "smart" garbage cans, to track what they throw into the trash. As the Internet of things grows, such concerns are sure to increase.

And that cascades into the fundamental privacy questions of big data. Should my employer be able to track the websites I'm visiting and the pace at which I complete online projects, to help feed big data analysis of work patterns and identify the most effective strategies for increasing productivity? Should private restaurant operators be worried that Yelp reviews, which are unscreened and which might or might not be accurate, are used to help target local governments' restaurant inspections? Government is not alone here. Google Trends tracks government searches from computers around the world, in real time. (As I write this paragraph on a Saturday afternoon in the fall, eight of the top ten Google searches deal with college football. The day before, however, the top search was for Edward Snowden.) Our cable companies know what we're watching on television, smartphone companies know what music we're listening to, and a feature on my smartphone knows where I parked my car (even though I didn't ask my phone to track it). Now, as is entirely possible, I might forget just where I left my car, and that map could prove very handy. But what broader use is—or could be—made of the rich data trail that all of us leave behind? What could government do with it? And what obligation does government have in protecting the way that others use these data?

These are questions for which, quite frankly, there are no good answers. In fact, this only scratches the surface of the puzzles lurking out there. But two things are certain. One is that these questions are only going to grow in number and importance as big data applications grow. The other is that the first step toward wrestling with them lies in transparency. Even if we don't know the answers, transparency can at least help us track and understand the questions.

Speaking above the Noise

The world of data is certain to be increasingly busy and noisy. There's simply no going back. The real challenge is keeping an eye on where we're going, how best to use the data we collect to make government work better, and how to make sure that we stay masters of that data—that we can hold the data accountable and not have the data rule us. We need sharp insights on these questions to help us speak above the noise and make sure that the data help us know better.

That's a deceptively tough problem. Harvard scholar Cass Sunstein and his colleagues set out to explore a basic question: If we share more information with citizens, do their opinions change? They applied this idea to a big and fundamental topic: climate change. They surveyed more than three hundred Americans on important climate change issues, like whether climate change caused by humans was real and whether the United States should have supported the 2016 Paris agreement to reduce greenhouse gases. "Do numbers and figures change people's opinions?" Sunstein and his co-investigators wondered. They looked carefully at the surveys and concluded, "Apparently, they do—they result in a deeper divide." We might expect that more and better research would produce stronger consensus. In fact, it sometimes only seems to increase political polarization.

In any analysis, there's usually good news and bad news. Supporters of a program tend to focus more on good news about it. Foes lean toward negative views of programs they oppose. Moreover, Sunstein and his team concluded, "As the sheer volume of information increases, polarization will be heightened as well." The good news behind this discouraging picture: most people are willing to look at data and, when they do so, they're willing to change their opinions, at least a little.[20]

And this takes us back to where we began in this book. There's often a strong belief that more and better information is the answer to many of the tough issues that government faces. Analysts, in particular, believe there ought to be more and better analysis. And, of course, on one level, it's hard to argue with that. Maya Angelou's powerful and poetic note, "Now that I know better, I do better," resonates through the work of policy analysis.

That ought to make the twenty-first century a golden era for government. The information age is sweeping us along and the volume of information, especially about the fundamental issues on which government focuses, is increasing in ways that are hard to keep up with or comprehend. Big data provides vast new opportunities to know more about new questions. Yet trust in government remains low and polarization has increased. Does that mean we ought to give up—or at least brush away any ethical concerns about simply providing whatever analysis best serves those willing to pay the most for it?

Fortunately, as we've seen in this book, we don't have to bite down on this cynical pill. Better information can often produce much more effective government. The road to doing that, however, isn't an easy one. It begins by remembering that those making decisions don't really need the information that analysts are producing. To be effective, that information has to be packaged in ways that are clear and persuasive, that supply answers to questions for which decision makers have demands, and that recognize that the process ultimately is a political one, not an analytical one. The great advances we've made in producing more and better statistical models surely help. But, to a degree often not appreciated, we can make big progress by taking little bites of big data. The story is a hopeful one, after all—at least for those with the skills and values to tell it.

Notes

1. Michigan Department of Transportation, "Bridges," http://www.michigan.gov/mdot/0,4616,7-151-13995-28274—F,00.html.

2. Kathleen Lavey, "Mackinac Bridge to Be Test Site for Stress Sensors," *Lansing State Journal* (September 3, 2016), http://www.lansingstatejournal.com/story/news/local/2016/09/03/mackinac-bridge-test-site-stress-sensors/89830524.

3. Lindsey Clark, "Waste and Traffic Management Apps Come from Internet of Things," *ComputerWeekly* (March 2015), http://www.computerweekly.com/feature/Waste-and-traffic-management-applications-come-from-Internet-of-Things.

4. "Dating App Technology Could Increase Local Voter Engagement" (August 23, 2016), https://www.youtube.com/watch?v=28wl7QOg91o.

5. Kimbriell Kelly, "Can Big Data Stop Bad Cops?" *Washington Post* (August 21, 2016), https://www.washingtonpost.com/investigations/can-big-data-stop-bad-cops/2016/08/21/12db0728-3fb6-11e6-a66f-aa6c1883b6b1_story.html?utm_term=.d7a4ebe379b6.

6. "Can Big Data Help Head Off Police Misconduct?" *National Public Radio* (July 19, 2016), http://www.npr.org/sections/alltechconsidered/2016/07/19/486499835/can-big-data-help-head-off-police-misconduct.

7. Bill Lucia, "As Child Welfare Agencies Turn to Data Analytics 'We Have to Be Really Careful'" *Route Fifty* (September 28, 2016), http://www.routefifty.com/2016/09/child-welfare-predictive-analytics/131897/?oref=rf-today-nl.

8. Alive Rivlin, *Systematic Thinking for Social Action,* new ed. (Washington, D.C.: Brookings Institution, 2015), xi.

9. "Ted Turner Quotes," Brainy Quote, http://www.brainyquote.com/quotes/quotes/t/tedturner162256.html.

10. Gregory Korte, "Even Obama's Motorcade Was Stalled by D.C. Snow," *USA Today* (January 21, 2016), http://www.usatoday.com/story/news/politics/theoval/2016/01/21/obamas-motorcade-also-stalled-dc-snow/79123558.

11. Fred Barbash and Justin Wm. Moyer, "An Inch of Snow, Icy Roads Unleash 9 Hours of Traffic Chaos across D.C. Region," *Washington Post* (January 21, 2016), https://www.washingtonpost.com/news/morning-mix/wp/2016/01/21/an-inch-of-snow-icy-roads-unleash-9-hours-of-traffic-chaos-across-d-c-region.

12. Dan Stillman, "Models Continue to Show Massive Snowstorm Starting Midday Friday," *Washington Post* (January 20, 2016), https://www.washington post.com/news/capital-weather-gang/wp/2016/01/20/model-live-blog-honing-in-on-the-details-of-a-huge-winter-storm.

13. Kathryn Zickuhr and Aaron Smith, "Home Broadband 2013" (Washington, DC: Pew Research Center, 2013), http://www.pewinternet.org/2013/08/26/home-broadband-2013.

14. Ibid.

15. Cathy O'Neil, "More Creepy Models," Mathbabe (September 13, 2016), https://mathbabe.org/2016/09/13/more-creepy-models-2.

16. Cathy O'Neil, *Weapons of Math Destruction: How Big Data Increases Inequality and Threatens Democracy* (New York: Crown, 2016).

17. Quoted by Priya Rao, "Math Is Biased against Women and the Poor, According to a Former Math Professor," *New York* (September 6, 2016), http://nymag.com/thecut/2016/09/cathy-oneils-weapons-of-math-destruction-math-is-biased.html.

18. Ibid.

19. Cass Sunstein and Reid Hastie, *Wiser: Getting beyond Groupthink to Make Groups Smarter* (Cambridge, MA: Harvard Business School Press, 2015); and Irving Janis, *Victims of Groupthink: A Psychological Study of Foreign-Policy Decisions and Fiascoes* (Boston: Houghton Mifflin, 1972).

20. Tali Shardt and Cass R. Sunstein, "Why Facts Don't Unify Us," *New York Times* (September 2, 2016), http://www.nytimes.com/2016/09/04/opinion/sunday/why-facts-dont-unify-us.html?_r=0.

• Index •